The Japanese Sword

Kanzan Satō

translated and adapted by

Joe Earle

Publication of this book was assisted by a grant from the Japan Foundation.

The editors wish to thank Susumu Kashima of Tokyo National Museum for his assistance with technical details. Plates 3, 5, 6, 7, 10, and 12 are based on or taken from Yūichi Hiroi, *Tōken no Mikata* (Tokyo: Dai-ichi Hōki, 1971).

The Japanese Sword was originally published in Japanese by the Shibundo publishing company, Tokyo, in 1966, under the title *Tōken*, as volume 6 in the series *Nihon no bijutsu*. The English edition was prepared at Kodansha International, Tokyo, by Saburo Nobuki, Yoko Takaya, Takako Suzuki, and Peter Goodman.

Library of Congress Cataloging in Publication Data

Satō, Kanzan, 1907–1978.
  The Japanese sword.

  (Japanese arts library; 12)
  Translation of: Tōken.
  Bibliography: p.
  Includes index.
  1. Swords—Japan. I. Earle, Joe. II. Title.
III. Series.
NK6784.A1S2413 1983   739.7′22′0952   82–48779
ISBN 0–87011–562–6 (U.S.)
First edition, 1983
Fifth printing, 1986   ISBN 4–7700–1055–9 (in Japan)

CONTENTS

ILLUSTRATIONS

Japanese Art Periods

Period	Sub-period	Dates	Range
Prehistoric			–537
Asuka			538–644
Nara			645–781
	Hakuhō	645–710	
	Tempyō	711–781	
Heian			782–1184
	Jōgan	782–897	
	Fujiwara	898–1184	
Kamakura			1185–1332
Nambokuchō			1333–91
Muromachi			1392–1572
Momoyama			1573–99
Edo			1600–1867
Meiji			1868–1912

Note: This table, compiled for the arts and crafts by the Agency for Cultural Affairs of the Japanese Government, has been adopted for general use in this series.

A Note to the Reader

Japanese names in the main text are given in the customary Japanese order, surname preceding given name.

INTRODUCTION

Japanese writers, however freely they may acknowledge their country's indebtedness to her mainland neighbors in other cultural fields, consistently stress the uniqueness of the Japanese sword. This uniqueness is not due to the mere continuation of a tradition in Japan which has died out in its country of origin, but to positive technical innovations devised by the Japanese themselves in an effort to resolve the three conflicting practical requirements of a sword: unbreakability, rigidity, and cutting power. Unbreakability implies a soft but tough metal, such as iron, which will not snap with a sudden blow, while rigidity and cutting power are best achieved by the use of hard steel. The Japanese have combined these features in a number of ways which have given their swords a very distinctive character.

First of all, most Japanese blades are made up of two different metals a soft and durable iron core is enveloped in a hard outer skin of steel which has been forged and reforged many times in order to produce a complex and close-knit crystalline structure. Second, the cross-section, widening from the back to a ridge on both sides, then narrowing to a very acute angle at the edge, combines the virtues of thickness for strength and thinness for cutting power. Third and most important of all, a highly tempered edge is formed by covering the rest of the blade with a special heat-resistant clay and heating and quenching only the part left exposed. The result is a steel which is even harder than the rest of the outer skin and can take a razor-sharp edge. A fourth feature, the distinctive curve away from the edge, owes its origin to another practical demand: the need to draw the sword and strike as quickly as possible and in a continuous motion. Where the sword itself forms part of the approximate circumference of a circle with its center at the wearer's right shoulder and its radius the length of his arm, drawing from a narrow scabbard will naturally be easier and faster than with a straight weapon.

But to the Japanese specialist the beauty of a sword lies in more than just its fulfillment of practical requirements or its almost mechanical perfection of finish and cleanness of profile. The Japanese swordsmith has given his product a number of features which, although they may have a strictly practical origin, have been elaborated far beyond the simple requirement of hard-wearing efficiency in slaughter. One

13

example of this is the forging of the outer skin, a process necessary to produce steel of adequate purity and hardness; this has been done in a multitude of different ways so as to obtain a wide variety of distinct grains in the surface of the blade. But it is the tempering process which has received the most careful attention. The heat-resistant clay is wholly or partially scraped away from the area of the edge in a seemingly inexhaustible range of outlines resulting in an enormous number of patterns of hard crystalline steel which guarantee that no two swords will ever be the same; and yet these outlines have no practical function beyond the simple requirement that the edge must be tempered in one way or another.

From a glance at a group of Japanese swords of about the same length and with the same basic cross-section it appears that the differences between them are very slight. To the uninitiated they may in fact be imperceptible, even if the swords have received the benefit of the very latest techniques of polishing. This is as true for the Japanese as for the Western layman. As a result, the study of Japanese blades has been and continues to be highly specialized. In the past, it was confined to a few families of hereditary experts, among whom the Hon'ami were preeminent, and it is significant that no less an artist than Hon'ami Kōetsu (1558–1637), the celebrated calligrapher, potter, and arbiter of Momoyama and early Edo townsman taste, should early in his career have trained in this most demanding of aesthetic disciplines. The full appreciation of a Japanese blade involves an understanding of every feature of its construction, from the outline of the tempered edge at the point to the style of the often barely visible filemarks on the part of the blade which, when it is mounted, lies completely hidden inside the hilt.

The long tradition of professional connoisseurship has resulted in the development of a bewildering universe of specialist terminology. In certain cases, it must be admitted, there was self-indulgent proliferation of words relating to some minute feature. But in general the very subtle distinctions which make one blade different from another amply justify the development of an exclusive vocabulary. The specialist language of swords is only the extreme example of a phenomenon which occurs in many of the other arts and crafts of Japan, and it might be argued that traditional experience in the accurate application and manipulation of such linguistic models is a feature of Japanese culture which has contributed much to the country's success in the modern industrial world.

When studying the indigenous scholarship of the Japanese sword, one is constantly struck by the writers' tendency to qualify even the well-developed vocabulary at their disposal. Thus we may find a *chū-kissaki* ("medium-length" point) described as "longish" or a *notare* (gently undulating) temper-line called "rather sharp." In fact, no clear distinction can be made between one term and its closest neighbor in meaning. In particular, words are often inadequate to describe the qualities of a really fine tempered edge, and writers are sometimes forced to convey something of their meaning by a simile drawn from the natural world, as in the case of the blade by Masamune

14

(pl. 67) discussed in chapter 2. The limited selection of about seventy-five Japanese terms which follows will give the reader some idea of the appearance of the standard types of blade as well as offer some further insight into the features of swords which most attract the specialist's attention. These terms, and other more specialized ones, are all listed alphabetically in the Glossary at the end of this book. Note also that the prefixes ō-, chū-, and ko- are often used to indicate degree, meaning "large," "moderate," and "small," respectively.

IMPORTANT FEATURES OF THE JAPANESE SWORD

TYPES OF BLADE

tachi: blade for a slung sword, worn edge downwards. The length, as defined below in "Parts of the Blade" under the term *nagasa*, is usually 70–80 centimeters.

katana (or *uchigatana*): blade for a sword which is worn edge upwards. The length of the *katana* blade is usually shorter than that of the *tachi*. Also, largely due to the style of mounted combat in earlier days, when armor was lighter and there was greater reliance on the bow and arrow, the *tachi* is generally lighter in weight in proportion to its length, shows a greater taper from hilt to point, is more curved, and has a smaller point area.

wakizashi: blade for a sword similar to the *katana*, but about two-thirds its length.

tantō: blade for any short sword, but generally considered to be limited to 30.5 centimeters.

PARTS OF THE BLADE

kissaki: the point of the blade, defined as the area beyond the *yokote*.

yokote: a small ridge at right angles to the main ridge (*shinogi*), marking off the *kissaki*.

shinogi: a ridge, on both sides of the blade, running the length of the blade from the *yokote*, usually nearer to the back (*mune*) than to the edge (*ha*).

ha: the tempered edge of the blade.

hamon: outline of the border between the tempered *ha* and the untempered metal of the rest of the blade; the temper-line.

bōshi: outline of the part of the *ha* which lies in the *kissaki*.

ji: area between the *ha* and the *shinogi*.

shinogiji: area between the *shinogi* and the *mune*.

mune: back of the blade; more specifically, its outline.

munamachi: notch in the back of the blade, defining the beginning of the tang (*nakago*).

hamachi: notch in the edge of the blade, opposite the *munamachi*, defining the beginning of the tang.

habakimoto: area covered by the *habaki*, a collar fitted over the blade between the tang and the polished part when the blade is mounted.

nakago: the unpolished part of the blade which goes inside the hilt when the blade is mounted, called in English the tang.

yasurime: filemarks on the tang, non-functional but varying from smith to smith and school to school and serving as a kind of additional signature.

mei: signature, if any, on the tang. In the case of *tachi*, it is on the side of the tang which faces away from the body when the sword is worn edge downwards, i.e., the side of the sword which has the edge to the right. In the case of *katana* it is on the opposite side.

nakagojiri: butt of the tang.

2.

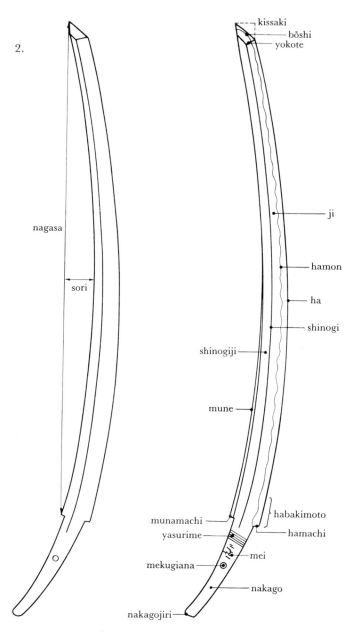

nagasa

sori

kissaki
bōshi
yokote

ji

hamon

ha

shinogi

shinogiji

mune

munamachi
yasurime

habakimoto
hamachi

mei

mekugiana

nakago

nakagojiri

mekugiana: hole for the retaining peg (*meku-gi*) which holds the tang in the hilt.

nagasa: length, defined as the length of the chord joining the point and the *munamachi*. All blade lengths given in this book are *nagasa* unless stated otherwise.

sori: curve, defined as the greatest perpen-dicular distance between the *nagasa*-chord and the *mune*.

sakihaba: width of the blade at the *yokote*.

motohaba: width of the blade at the *habaki-moto*. The term *fumbari* is used to indicate that a blade is considerably wider at its *motohaba* than at its *sakihaba*.

16

3.

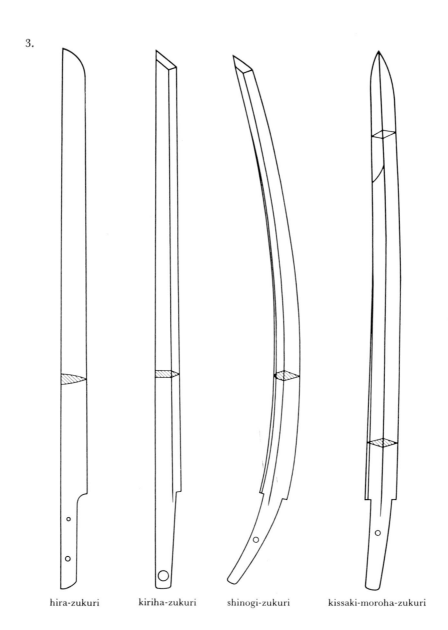

hira-zukuri   kiriha-zukuri   shinogi-zukuri   kissaki-moroha-zukuri

TYPES OF BLADE CROSS-SECTION

hira-zukuri: flat with no ridge, roughly triangular in cross-section.

kiriha-zukuri: with flat sides, but with a tapering angle between the sides and the *ha*.

shinogi-zukuri: widening to a ridge which is nearer the *mune* than the *ha*, then narrowing to the *ha*.

kissaki-moroha-zukuri (or *kogarasu-zukuri*): double-edged near the point and single-edged near the hilt, with a ridge running lengthwise in the center of the blade.

17

4.

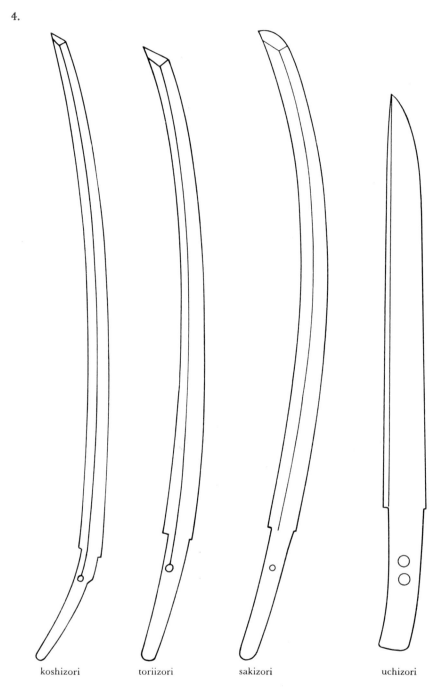

koshizori   toriizori   sakizori   uchizori

TYPES OF CURVE

koshizori: with the center of the curve near the tang or in the tang.

toriizori: with the center of the curve roughly in the center of the blade.

sakizori: with the center of the curve near the point of the blade.

uchizori: a slight curve towards, rather than away from, the edge.

5.

TYPES OF BLADE BACK
iorimune: ridged.
marumune: rounded.
mitsumune: three-sided.

iorimune   marumune   mitsumune

6.

 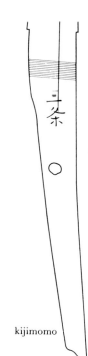

funagata

TYPES OF TANG
funagata: short and stubby; the name suggests the profile of a Japanese fishing boat.
kijimomo: narrowing sharply on the edge side. Literally, "pheasant's thigh."
ubu: does not refer to shape, but denotes a tang whose butt and *machi* (i.e., *hamachi* and *munamachi*) are in their original location and condition. The tang may still be called *ubu* even if it has been slightly reshaped or drilled with extra *mekugiana* because of remounting.

kijimomo

7.

 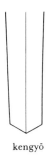 

TYPES OF BUTT
iriyamagata: asymmetrical V-shape.
kengyō: symmetrical V-shape.
kurijiri: rounded asymmetrical V-shape.

iriyamagata   kengyō   kurijiri

19

8.

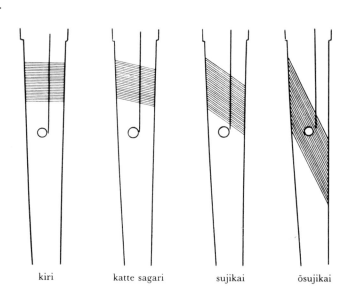

kiri   katte sagari   sujikai   ōsujikai

TYPES OF FILEMARK

kiri: at right angles to the length of the tang.

katte sagari: sloping slightly towards the back of the tang.

sujikai: sloping towards the back of the tang, more than *katte sagari*.

ōsujikai: sloping towards the back of the tang, more than *sujikai*.

9.

ko-kissaki   chū-kissaki   ikubi-kissaki

TYPES OF POINT

ko-kissaki: short in proportion to the width of the blade near the tang.

chū-kissaki: of medium length in proportion to the width of the blade near the tang.

ikubi-kissaki: like *ko-kissaki*, but somewhat stubby. Literally, like a wild boar's neck.

20

10.

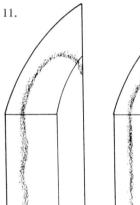 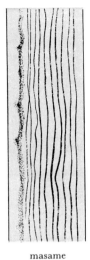  

| itame | masame | mokume | ayasugihada |

TYPES OF GRAIN IN THE JI

itame: wood-grain, resembling the surface of a wooden board cut against the grain. *Nagare itame* is a spirally variation.

ko-itame: fine *itame* grain.

masame: straight grain with lines running parallel to the length of the blade.

mokume: burl wood-grain.

ayasugihada: regular, concentric, and wavy, resembling woodgrain of the *sugi* (cryptomeria) tree.

11.

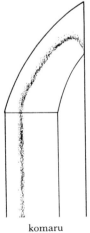 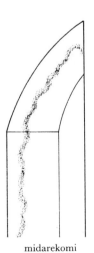 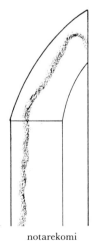 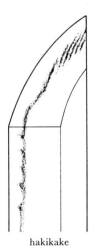

| ōmaru | komaru | midarekomi | notarekomi | hakikake |

FEATURES OF THE BŌSHI

ōmaru: large, sweeping turnback of the *hamon* in the *kissaki*.

komaru: small turnback at the end.

midarekomi: continuing the irregularity of the main *hamon* into the point.

notarekomi: continuing the gentle undulations of the main *hamon* into the point.

hakikake: swept or brushstroke pattern of *nie* (see under "Features of the *Ha* and *Ji*," below).

21

12.

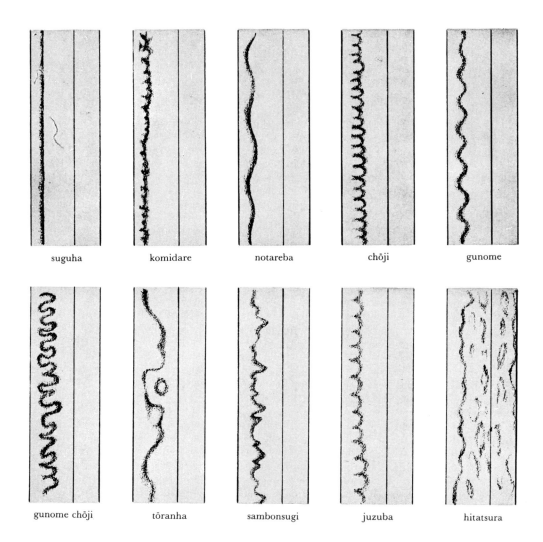

suguha komidare notareba chōji gunome

gunome chōji tōranha sambonsugi juzuba hitatsura

TYPES OF HAMON

suguha: straight. The term *chū-suguha* is used with a *ha* of medium width, *hososuguha* with a narrow *ha*, and *ito suguha* with a very narrow *ha*.

midareba: irregular. *Komidare* has small, frequent irregularities; *ōmidare* has large, less frequent irregularities.

notareba: gently undulating. In *konotare* the undulations are small and frequent, in *ōnotare* they are large and less frequent.

chōji: irregular, with lines from the *hamon* extending into the *ha*.

gunome: an outline consisting of small pointed curves.

gunome chōji: combining *chōji* and *gunome*.

tōranha: very large, irregular outline.

sambonsugi: sharply undulating, with undulations in groups of three, some deeper than others.

juzuba: similar to *chōji*. For the difference, see the sketch.

hitatsura: with tempering marks visible around the ridge as well as near the edge of the blade.

13.

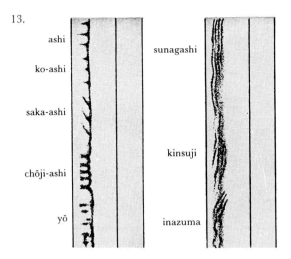

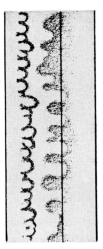

ashi

ko-ashi

saka-ashi

chōji-ashi

yō

sunagashi

kinsuji

inazuma

utsuri

FEATURES OF THE HA AND JI

nie, nioi: hard bright areas of steel of martensitic crystalline structure, resulting from the tempering process and forming the *hamon* by standing out in contrast to areas of softer pearlitic structure. When individual and discrete, called *nie*; when appearing like mist or clouds, called *nioi*. These and the other features listed below cannot really be shown in a sketch and are only visible upon close examination of the metal under proper lighting conditions.

konie: small *nie*.

jinie: *nie* occurring in the *ji* rather than the *ha*.

chikei: brightly shining lines in the *ji*.

ashi: wedged-shaped areas of martensitic structure projecting into the *ha* at right angles to the *hamon*. *Ko-ashi*, *saka-ashi*, and *chōji-ashi* are typical variants (see the sketch).

yō: detached, leaf-shaped *ashi* in the *hamon*.

sunagashi: lines of *nie* in the *ha*, parallel to the *hamon*.

kinsuji: like *chikei* but occurring in the *ha*. *Inazuma* is an angular variant.

utsuri: cloudy area of bright crystalline metal bordering the *hamon* and often appearing to be a reflection of it in the *ji*. It is separated from the *hamon* by a darker area of non-reflective quality.

THE FIVE TRADITIONS OF SWORD MANUFACTURE

Each of the Five Traditions (*gokaden*) of Yamashiro, Sagami, Bizen, Yamato, and Mino takes its name from a province which has been important in the history of sword manufacture (the tradition of Sagami province has conventionally been called Sōshū-den rather than Sagami-den, taking another of the province's names, but this confusing anomaly has been ignored in the present translation). These traditions are indicative only of general stylistic trends, and many conflicting trends may coexist within one tradition, but they are still frequently referred to today. They have considerable validity for the so-called Kotō ("Old Sword") period, which lasted until the end of the sixteenth century, but the development at that time of communications and of economic activity in general led many smiths to move to the great urban centers or into the service of regional military rulers (*daimyō*) throughout Japan, with the result that the old provincial styles can no longer be distinguished in the Shintō ("New Sword") period, which lasted until the end of the eighteenth century. However,

23

in the Shinshintō ("New-New Sword") period, which lasted until the abolition of sword-wearing in 1876, there was a move towards conscious imitation of Kamakura-period styles and, as a result, the Five Traditions regained something of their old significance. A brief account of these traditions will serve as a broad introduction to the history of the Japanese sword until about 1600, and it will illustrate the way in which one school could influence another. It will also show how the specialist vocabulary is used to build up a stylistic picture of the work of a smith or group of smiths.

Yamashiro

The earliest smith working at Kyoto in Yamashiro province whose name we know is Sanjō Munechika. His *tachi*, signed *Sanjō* (after the name of a street in Kyoto) or *Munechika*, are generally thought to date from the tenth century. They have a deep *koshizori* curve and exemplify the feature known as *fumbari*: greater width at the hilt end (*motohaba*) than at the point end (*sakihaba*). His *kissaki* are short (*ko-kissaki*), the grain is *koitame*, and the *hamon*, made up of both *nie* and *nioi*, is sometimes *ko-midare* and sometimes double (*nijūha*) or even treble (*sanjūha*). A later very important school is the Awataguchi, named after the Awataguchi district of Kyoto. Its leading members include Kunitomo (late twelfth to early thirteenth century), whose *tachi* are similar to those of Munechika but usually have a *suguha hamon* in combination with *komidare*, and Tōshirō Yoshimitsu, one of the most celebrated of all smiths, whose *tantō*, ranging in length from about 20 to about 30 centimeters, are in *hira-zukuri* form, with *uchizori*, *koitame* grain, usually a basically *suguha hamon*, and a long tang with *kurijiri* butt and gently sloping *katte sagari* filemarks. A third Yamashiro group is the Rai school. The blades of the true founder, Kuniyuki (thirteenth century), are chiefly *tachi* and are of two types, broad and narrow, with a *chōji* or *komidare hamon* made up of both *nie* and *nioi* and *itame* grain. Later, in the work of Rai Kunimitsu (early fourteenth century), *gunome hamon* are found as a result of influence from the Sagami tradition.

Sagami

The Sagami or Sōshū tradition owes its origins to the patronage of the military government following the choice of Kamakura, in Sagami province, near modern Tokyo, as the seat of the *bakufu* set up by the military overlord, or *shōgun*, Minamoto no Yoritomo (1147–99) in 1185. It may be said to begin in 1249, when Awataguchi Kunitsuna, a scion of the Yamashiro tradition, came to Kamakura and forged a *tachi* for the Hōjō regent Tokiyori (1227–63). Kunitsuna's son, Shintōgo Kunimitsu, was the teacher of Yukimitsu and of the great Masamune, who is generally regarded as the outstanding exponent of the Sagami tradition and indeed of sword-making in general. As the author indicates in chapter 1, *tantō* (short swords) came into widespread currency after the two attempted invasions by the Mongol fleet in the later thirteenth century and, appropriately enough, *tantō* constitute the most characteristic products of the tradition, although important long swords, both *tachi* and *katana*, were also made. These *tantō* are usually from about 24 to about 28 centimeters long (with the exception of the shorter and wider so-called "kitchen-knife" [*hōchō*] *tantō*; see pl. 67) and have either no curve at all or slight *uchizori*. The grain is most often a very fine and compact *itame*, and the *hamon*, which are various but in the case of Masamune usually *midareba*, are made up of very bright and active *nie*.

Bizen

Bizen province on the Inland Sea, corresponding roughly with present-day Okayama Prefecture, has been a center of iron production since early times. From the late Heian period until the disastrous floodings of the Yoshii River in the late sixteenth century the area centering on the town of Osafune was perhaps the most prolific source of sword blades in the whole of Japan. The three great names among the smiths of the so-called Ko-Bizen ("Old Bizen") school, which flourished in the late Heian period (tenth to twelfth centuries) are Tomonari, Masatsune, and Kanehira. Their *tachi* are generally thin (with the exception of a few blades like the magnificent Ō-Kanehira; see pl. 59) with strong *koshizori* and *ko-kissaki*. The grain is *itame* or *koitame* and the *hamon* is mainly *komidare* made up of *nie*, in combination with *chōji* and *gunome*. In the thirteenth century the Heian style was maintained by the Ichimonji, founded by Norimune (see pl. 61), and Osafune schools, but later, blades became wider and the *kissaki* longer, a practical development probably reflecting experience gained from fighting the Mongols with their thick leather armor. In the work of the Osafune school the curve moved from the hilt (*koshizori*) towards the middle of the blade (*toriizori*) and in the fourteenth century *tachi* became still longer and wider and the influence of the Sagami tradition was briefly felt in gentler *hamon* such as *notare* and *ōmidare*. Early in the Muromachi period some fine *tachi* were produced with the very distinctive *gunome chōji hamon*, but the heavy demand for swords in the troubled years from the early fifteenth century to the end of the sixteenth century made Bizen, with Mino, one of the two great centers of mass-production, chiefly of *katana*, both for the home market and for bulk exports to China. Few swords of any distinction were made, the only exceptions being a number of special orders, an example of which is shown in plate 69.

Yamato

The Yamato tradition is the oldest of all, starting with the emergence of the province as the political center of Japan in the fourth century A.D. and the introduction of ironworking techniques from China. Amakuni, a semi-legendary figure who has been called the father of the Japanese sword, is said to have been a native of Yamato province and to have lived in the early eighth century, but this account is not accepted today. The character of Yamato blades before the appearance from the twelfth century onwards of the "Five Schools" (Senjuin, Taima, Tekai, Shikkake, and Hōshō) may

25

only be guessed at, but in the Kamakura period a clearer picture emerges. The ridge is high, the grain is *masame* or *itame*, the basic *hamon* is *suguha* made up of *nie* and sometimes combined with *midare*. Unlike the Bizen and Yamashiro traditions, there are usually no *chōji* in the *hamon* and as a rule the extremely bright and active *nie* of the Sagami tradition are not found. In general, the style of Yamato blades is restrained, conservative, and static. The history of sword manufacture in Yamato province is intimately associated with the old temples of Nara and elsewhere, whose monks were fierce participants in warfare, and it was through the medium of these temples' great estates in other provinces and the trading activities of the monks that "Nara swords" (*Nara-tō*) became known throughout Japan during the Kamakura period. The Tekai school is of particular importance for the fact that its members included Kaneuji, who moved to Shizu in Mino province and founded the Mino tradition at the very end of the Kamakura period.

Mino

Kaneuji's *tachi* are normally of standard width with a *kissaki* of standard length, and the filemarks on his tangs are either right-angled *kiri* or the slightly sloping *katte sagari*, like those of Sagami, where Kaneuji studied under Masamune. The features of his blades which later became characteristic of the Mino style include the combination of *itame* with *masame*, *jinie* and *chikei* in the *ji*, a *komidare hamon* with a somewhat *gunome* feel (derived from Yamato) or a *notare hamon* (derived from Masamune). The *hamon* is made up of *nie*, with *sunagashi* and *hakikake* in the *ha*. Among the seven groups which make up the tradition, the school of Yoshisada and Kaneyoshi (late fourteenth to early fifteenth century) has the clearest individual character, especially because of its *hososuguha hamon*. In the Muromachi period, Seki in Mino and Osafune in Bizen were the greatest centers of sword production. The mass-produced blades of Seki were somewhat lacking in individual character, but not to the same extent as those of Osafune. A few smiths, or rather signatures representing groups of smiths, for example Kanesada and Kanemoto, made use of expressive *hamon* such as *sambonsugi*; this special emphasis on *hamon* became more pronounced as time went on and became a feature of the work of many swordsmiths of the early Edo period. In fact the majority of the new schools which arose during the Momoyama and early Edo periods have a Mino origin.

The author of this introductory study, Dr. Kanzan (or Kan'ichi) Satō (1907–78), is one of a small band of men who maintained the tradition of sword scholarship in the earlier part of the present Shōwa era. In particular, he and Dr. Junji Homma were largely responsible for persuading the American forces occupying Japan after the war of the artistic and spiritual, rather than purely practical and military, qualities of the Japanese sword, thereby saving a great many blades from destruction. In the rather easier years of the 1950s and 1960s he was active, as a leading member of the Agency for Cultural Affairs of the Japanese Government and the Society for the Preservation of Japanese Art Swords, in the study, registration, and preservation of Japan's sword heritage.

In his book Satō has relied to a considerable degree on the traditional method of teaching by example. Introducing the reader to a number of Japan's most famous blades and discussing their technical features, stylistic relationships, and often colorful historical background, he makes it possible to experience, albeit at second hand, the many levels of appreciation involved in the understanding and enjoyment of a fine sword. Of course there can be no substitute for direct examination, or for the sophisticated explanations of a specialist drawing on a lifetime's experience and communicating his enthusiasm for a sword as he holds it, but the commentarial method adopted here, formally in the second chapter, on fine swords, and by implication elsewhere, has been applied to every field of intellectual endeavor in the countries of the Far East for over two millennia and has immense historical authority. It is by the close and systematic study of individual specimens implied by such an approach that Dr. Satō and others like him have gained their unique insights. While younger men may give more weight to social and economic background, their preoccupations can never displace the informed connoisseurship of the previous generation of specialists.

The translator's thanks are due first of all to B. W. Robinson, formerly Keeper of the Department of Metalwork of the Victoria and Albert Museum, whose lifetime of profound scholarship and stalwart advocacy of the Japanese sword and its fittings have done so much to revive British public interest in the subject since the war. Ever generous of his knowledge, Mr. Robinson guided the translator's first studies in the field. Dr. Walter A. Compton, the greatest non-Japanese collector of Japanese swords, has acted as supervisor. He kindly read through the entire text in draft and made a number of valuable suggestions.

Joe Earle

1

THE DEVELOPMENT
OF THE JAPANESE SWORD

It was probably after the Stone Age and during the Iron Age that techniques of sword manufacture were first introduced to Japan from the mainland of Asia. It is not clear exactly when this happened but from an examination of the swords which have been excavated from tumuli all over Japan archeologists have suggested the fourth century A.D. as a likely upper limit. Of course swords probably existed before the fourth century but it was around that time that they came into widespread use.

Swords of this early period, called *jōkotō*, were straight (or rather lacked a deliberate curve). Evidence about their length can be found in the *Kojiki* and the *Nihon shoki*, two important historical works dating from 712 and 720, respectively, which include scattered references to swords of ten, nine, and eight "fists." The fist, defined as the distance that can be covered by four fingers, was used as a unit of length in early times. In practice, since fingers vary in thickness, the length of a fist would differ slightly depending on the size of hand, but 9 to 10 centimeters is probably standard. Therefore a "ten fist" sword would be some 90 centimeters to 1 meter long. The use of special units to measure these swords perhaps suggests that there was something unusual about their quality and size, and this is borne out by the fact that there are very few swords as long as this among those excavated from tumuli although there are many examples between 60 and 70 centimeters in length. Fifty-five swords of eighth century date survive in the Shōsō-in, a repository of art treasures built at Nara in the mid-eighth century; of these only one is over a meter long and the others are all under 90 centimeters, the majority of them being in the 60- to 70-centimeter range mentioned above. It seems reasonable to assume from these two groups of examples that the same proportions hold good for all swords produced at the time. These straight swords were worn slung from the waist and were used on foot; they served both as stabbing and as slashing weapons.

TACHI

The word *tachi*, the general term for the basic blade at this time, probably derives from *tachikiru*, "to cut in two," but in the *Tōdai-ji kemmotsuchō*, a register of objects

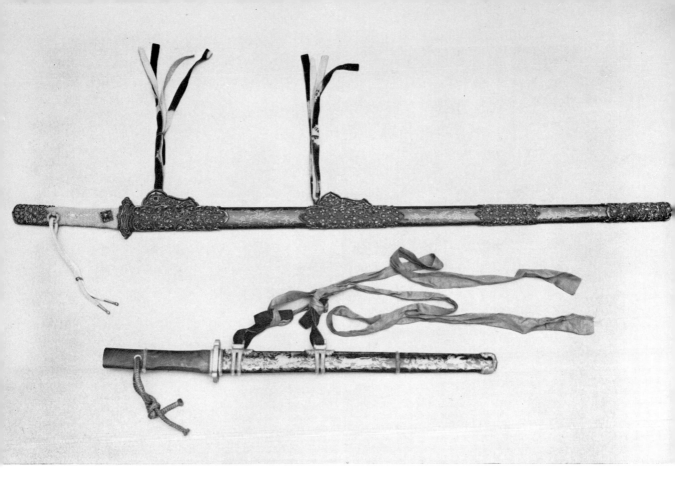

14. Reproductions of mountings in the Shōsō-in, Nara. ABOVE: *Kinginden sō no karatachi koshirae.* Chinese *tachi* mounting decorated in gold, silver, and mother-of-pearl. L. 102.0 cm. BELOW: *Kin heidatsu tachi koshirae. Tachi* mounting decorated in cut gold foil embedded in lacquer. L. 55.7 cm. Originals Nara period. Tokyo National Museum.

deposited by the emperor at the Shōsō-in, it is written with several different pairs of characters, the two main meanings being "great sword" and "horizontal sword." The characters meaning "great sword" seem to refer to swords over 60 centimeters in length while the characters meaning "horizontal sword" are used for shorter weapons.

The mounts attached to these *tachi* were all designed to be worn slung from a belt and because they hung horizontally the character meaning "horizontal" came to be used in connection with them. Such mounts were fashionable from the fourth to the ninth century and were only worn by persons of comparatively high rank. Some were imported from China and Korea while others were copies made in Japan, as can be seen from references in the *Tōdai-ji kemmotsuchō* to "T'ang *tachi*" and "Korean *tachi*" as well as "T'ang-style *tachi*." All these expressions can be taken as referring to mount and blade as a single unit. Although their function was primarily ceremonial these *tachi* were also practical weapons.

It is not known precisely how these *tachi* were used but it is probably safe to assume that they were wielded with one hand only. There is a mirror in the Shōsō-in whose back is decorated with figures in a boat brandishing in one hand swords of the *kantō no tachi* (ring-headed *tachi*) type illustrated in plate 18 and discussed in chapter 3.

The early *tachi* in the Shōsō-in include an unusually short example with a red wooden hilt and a scabbard decorated in a technique known as *heidatsu*, in which fine patterns in cut gold foil are covered in lacquer which is afterwards polished down so that the gold is visible under a thin layer of lacquer (pl. 14). Another type found in

29

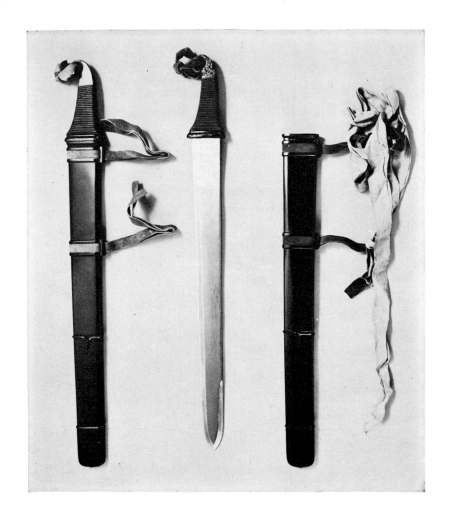

15. Reproductions of *warabite no tachi* ("young bracken frond" *tachi*) in the Shōsō-in, Nara. Scabbard black-lacquered leather wrapping; hilt wood. L. of blade on left 62.2 cm. Originals Nara period. Tokyo National Museum.

the Shōsō-in is the *warabite no tachi* ("young bracken frond" *tachi*), so called from the shape of the end of the hilt (pl. 15). It is obvious, to judge by the plain mounts and hilt of the *warabite no tachi*, that it was designed to be wielded with one hand and that it was intended for use by persons inferior in rank to those who wore the fully fitted *tachi* for which the characters meaning "great sword" are used. *Warabite no tachi* have been excavated throughout the country from Kyushu to Hokkaido but the Shōsō-in example is the only one to have been handed down from early times.

TSURUGI AND TSURUGI NO TACHI

The term *tsurugi* refers to a type of two-edged sword with a sharp point. It is not clear what it looked like in the early stages of its development but surviving examples from the period under discussion and later are symmetrical, with each edge the same or nearly the same distance from the central ridge. The expression *tsurugi no tachi* is often mentioned in the mid-eighth century *Man'yōshū* and other early verse collections, and it is explained as referring to a type of sword which has one edge in the part near the hilt and is two-edged only near the point. In the *Tōdai-ji kemmotsuchō* this type of sword is described as *kissaki-moroha-zukuri* ("two-edges-at-the-point style"). It was in vogue from the Nara period to the early part of the Heian period, that is, from the mid-seventh to the ninth century. Plate 16 shows the type of *tsurugi* (also called *ken*)

30

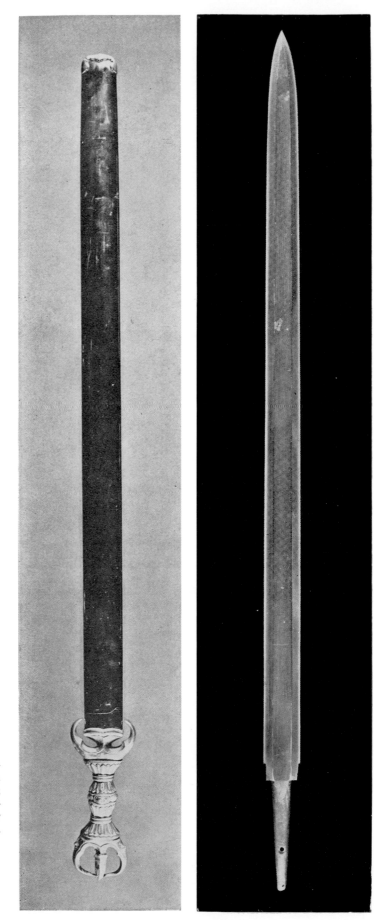

16. *Sanko-zuka tsurugi* (or *ken*). Double-edged sword with handle in the form of a Buddhist ritual implement. Steel; scabbard black-lacquered; handle gilt-bronze. *Nagasa* 62.2 cm. Blade early Heian period; mount Kamakura period. Kongō-ji, Osaka.

17. "Kogarasu-maru." *Tachi* attributed to Amakuni. Steel. *Nagasa* 62.8 cm. Early Heian period. Imperial Household Collection.

commonly found in sculptures of Buddhist deities such as the fierce figure of Fudō.

The celebrated sword called Kogarasu-maru ("The Little Crow"; pl. 17), an heir-loom of the Taira clan, was made, according to an old tradition, by a smith called Amakuni, and because it is in the two-edged *kissaki-moroha* style that style is sometimes also referred to as *kogarasu-zukuri* ("little crow style"). This Amakuni is said in old sword books to have lived in Yamato province at the beginning of the eighth century, but no signed examples of his work survive today. The *tachi* Kogarasu-maru, passed down from generation to generation in the Taira clan, is now in the Imperial Household Collection; although it is in the two-edged style it differs considerably in form and construction from the examples in the Shōsō-in in that, among other things, the blade is strongly curved near the hilt and the two-edged section is remark-ably long. To judge from the texture of the metal and the long groove carved along the blade, more appropriate to a halberd (*naginata*; see below) than to a sword, it is more likely to be of late eighth or early ninth century date.

18. *Kantō no tachi*. Wood with gilt bronze fittings. L. 100.0 cm. Kofun period. Tokyo National Museum.

Kantō no tachi—or *tachi* with ring pommels—have been excavated in considerable quantities all over Japan, but with the exception of a single example which has been handed down in the Komura Shrine, Kōchi Prefecture, the one shown here is in the best state of preservation. It is impossible to tell whether it is a native Japanese product or an import from the Asian mainland. The ring pommel is an exclusive feature of this style, but the other fittings, in particular the rudimentary guard and the two bands by which the sword was slung, developed rapidly in the following centuries and are found in one form or another on all subsequent *tachi*.

19. Reproduction of a portrait of Asa Taishi or Shō-toku Taishi. Ink, color, and gold on paper. H. 102.0 cm. Original seventh or eighth century. Imperial Household Collection.

Unfortunately it is not known whether the style of dress shown in this portrait reflects native Japanese or continental taste. Although it is clear that the decorative features of the mountings have been greatly exaggerated, the painting provides valuable evidence for the appearance of the swords worn by the emperor and nobility in the Asuka and early Nara periods.

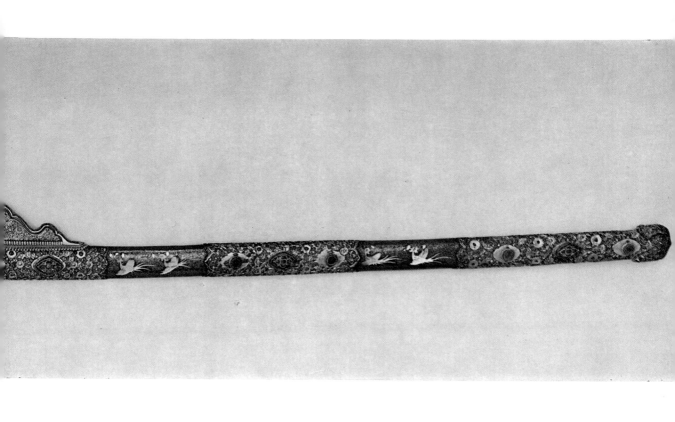

20–21. *Kazaritachi*. Mother-of-pearl (*raden*) on a ground of gold lacquer, with openwork gilt metal fittings and hilt wrapped in rayskin. L. 104.0 cm. Heian period. Tokyo National Museum.

The combination of an unwrapped rayskin hilt with a scabbard decorated in gold lacquer with mother-of-pearl inlay and elaborate gilt openwork embellished with enamels (missing in this example) is typical of aristocratic taste in the Heian period. This style continued in use until the Edo period.

22–23. *Tachi* mounting. Wood covered in a silvered copper band and with gilt bronze mounts. L. 104.0 cm. Heian period. Nibutsu-hime Shrine, Wakayama Prefecture. An example of the narrow *tachi* with a strong curve in or near the hilt typical of the Heian period. The technique of winding a silvered copper band round the scabbard is highly unusual.

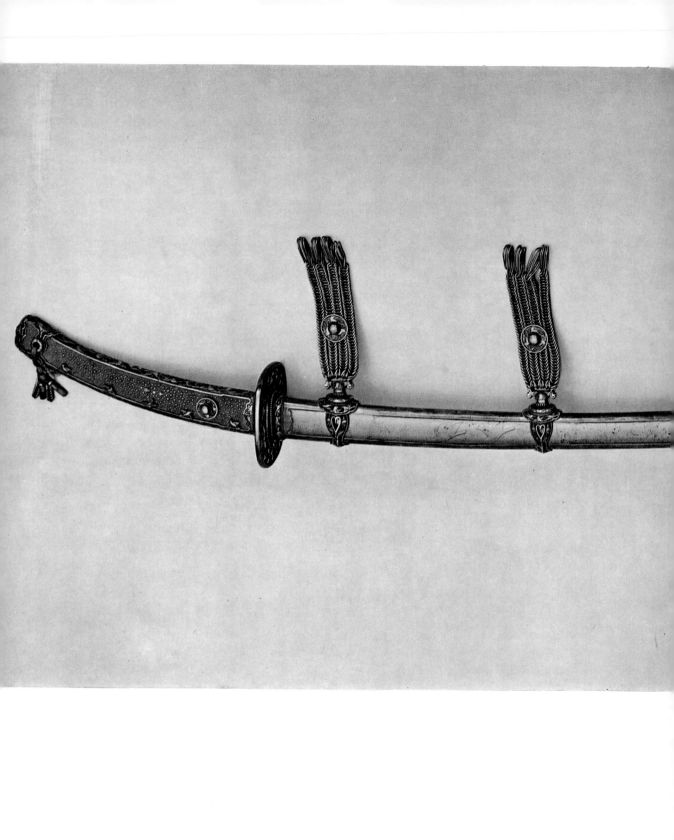

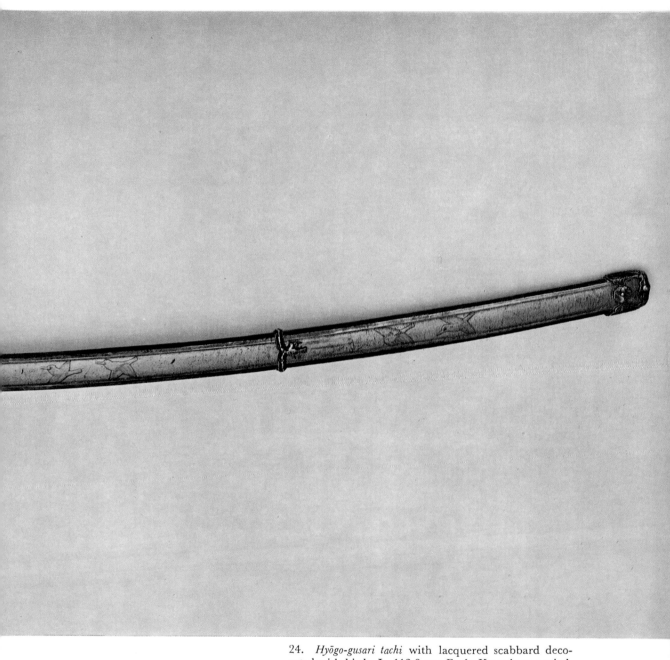

24. *Hyōgo-gusari tachi* with lacquered scabbard decorated with birds. L. 113.0 cm. Early Kamakura period.
Tokyo National Museum.

Both hilt and scabbard are fitted with a decorative silver
rim and the washers of the guard are pierced with a
design of a flock of birds. The gold lacquer ground of
the scabbard is decorated with the same design in
takamakie (relief lacquer). The use of this technique,
which was not known until the Kamakura period, provides further evidence that this style of slinging the sword
from woven chains came into fashion at the end of the
Heian and beginning of the Kamakura period.

25. Reproduction of a detail from the *Matsuzaki tenjin engi* picture scroll in Bōfu Shrine, Yamaguchi Prefecture. Ink, color, and gold on paper. Original anonymous, late thirteenth century. Tokyo National Museum.

One of the colophons to this picture scroll is dated to the Kōan period (1278–88). It shows a provincial governor holding a *nagafukurin hyōgo-gusari no tachi*, indicating that the style—with its long ornamental border—was in vogue among senior samurai towards the end of the thirteenth century.

Tōsu

A *tōsu* is a type of small knife. In the section of the *Nihon shoki* covering the fourth year of the reign of Emperor Suinin (26 B.C. according to tradition) there is a reference to a "small sword with a thread." There are two theories about this thread: according to one it was wrapped around the scabbard and hilt to prevent the blade being drawn inadvertently, while according to the other it was used to sling the sword from a belt at the waist. The latter explanation seems more likely, and what is described here is probably a prototype of the slings which were an important feature of many later sword mountings. Another term found in early sources is "eight-fold small knife with a thread," which was probably intended to draw attention to the sharpness of the blade by stressing that it had been hammered out and folded over many times during the process of forging.

We can tell from the *Nihon shoki* account, in which the "small knife" is used in an attempt on Emperor Suinin's life, that it was intended for practical use and was small enough to be carried secretly. References in the *Taihōryō* of 701 and other law codes suggest that *tōsu* were also symbols of rank and that they were worn by women of high rank as well as men. In the Shōsō-in there are sets of three (pl. 26) and ten (pl. 27) containing chisels and planes as well as simple knives. In all, about seventy *tōsu* survive in the Shōsō-in, ranging in blade length from 3 to 10 centimeters. Few others survive from that period and those that have been excavated are longer, with fine and elaborate mounts, calling to mind the *tantō* (short sword; see below) of later times. Similar swords have been excavated on the mainland, indicating that they are not a Japanese invention.

43

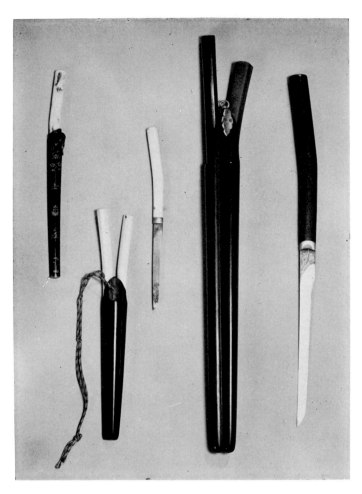

26. Reproductions of sets of three *tōsu* in the Shōsō-in, Nara. Wood, ivory, steel, gilt fittings. L. of set on right 25.0 cm. Originals Nara period. Tokyo National Museum.

27. Reproduction of a set of ten *tōsu* in the Shōsō-in, Nara. Wood and steel. L. 36.5 cm. Originals Nara period. Tokyo National Museum.

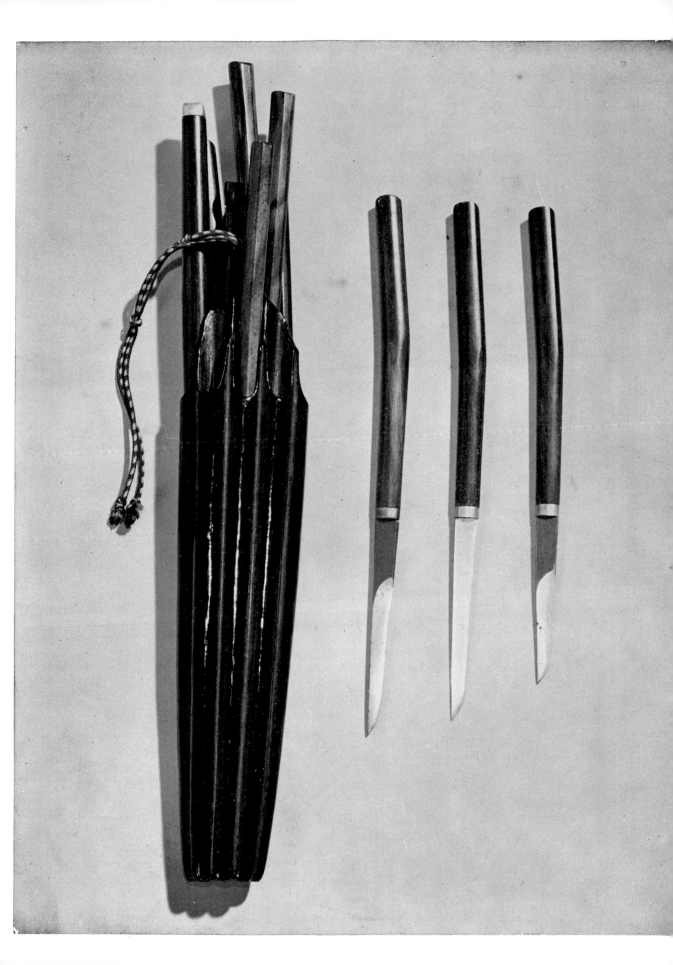

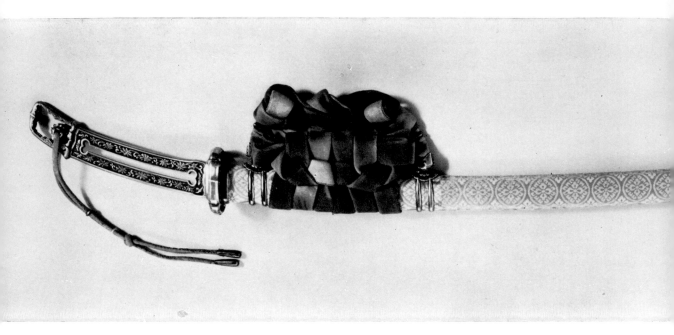

FROM THE STRAIGHT SWORD TO THE CURVED SWORD

Evidence for the date of the transition from straight to curved sword is afforded by the collections in the Shōsō-in, where we find that there are already some which have a deliberately produced, rather than a naturally occurring, curve. The introduction of the practice of imparting curves to blades shows us that sweeping strokes were now more important than stabbing lunges; this change clearly took place because sweeping strokes were vital to the warrior fighting on horseback rather than on foot. Among examples of swords representing a transitional stage between the straight and curved styles are the Kogarasu-maru *tachi* mentioned above and the *kenukigata no tachi* ("hair-tweezer shape," so called from the outline of the piercing in its hilt) illustrated in plate 28 and shown in use in the portrait reproduced in plates 83 and 84. These have only a slight curve in the main part of the blade but there is a sharp bend in the hilt so that the sword as a whole has a quite strongly curved appearance. Even this small development was a great asset from a practical point of view, but it now became necessary to impart a curve to the blade itself.

46   It might seem to the layman that no particular skill is required to give a blade

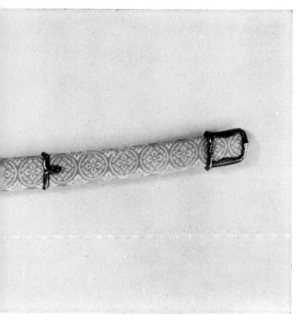

28. Reproduction of a *kenukigata no tachi* in the Chō-kokan at Ise, Mie Prefecture, said to have been used by Tawara Tōda Hidesato. Scabbard wood wrapped in brocade; hilt raised inlay on *nanako* (granulated) silver. L. 93.9 cm. Original mid-Heian period. Tokyo National Museum.

a strong or a slight curve. In fact it is a considerable technical feat. As the smith hammers one edge of his strip of metal out thin to form the edge of the blade, the thicker side tends to curve towards the thin side; to reverse this process and give the sword a deliberate curve requires a high level of skill and ingenuity. Furthermore, it is no easy task to curve the body of a blade near the hilt while at the same time giving a slight curve to the hilt itself, and so from necessity rather than choice the curve later came to be placed near the center of the blade or at its point.

An important aspect of the change from straight to curved swords is the development of a ridge construction (pl. 29). The earliest swords lacked a ridge, and while there is nothing wrong with a flat-sided (*hira-zukuri*) sword as far as simple sharpness goes, during forging the smith may have difficulty controlling the thickness of its metal. Too much metal will result in what is called a "clam edge" (*hamaguri ha*), in which the angle forming the edge of the blade is insufficiently acute, with the result that the sword, however strong it may be because of the thickness of its metal, may yet have an inferior cutting edge. If, on the other hand, the edge is too thin, the blade may be sharp but it is likely to bend or break.

47

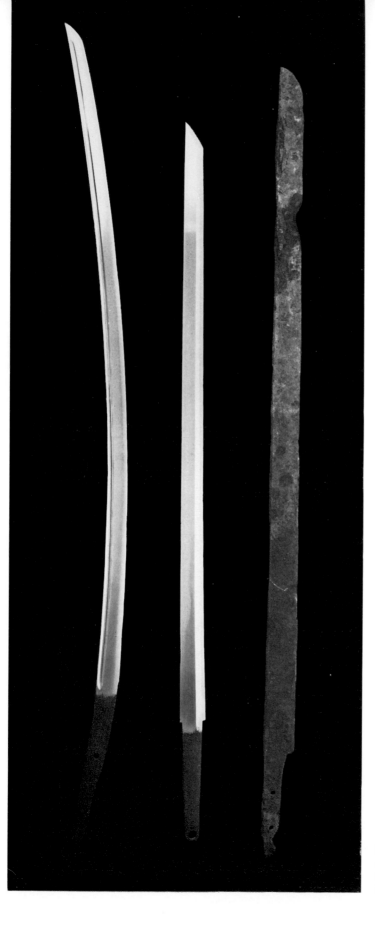

29.   Examples of different *tachi*. RIGHT:
Hira-zukuri.   CENTER: *Kinha-zukuri*.
LEFT: Curved *shinogi-zukuri*. Steel. To-
kyo National Museum.

(*Overleaf*)
30. Example of a straight *kiriha-zukuri tachi* originally in the Shōsō-in, Nara. Steel. *Nagasa* 62.2 cm. Nara period. Tokyo National Museum.

31. *Kiriha-zukuri tachi.* Steel. *Nagasa* 223.5 cm. Early Heian period. Kashima Shrine, Ibaraki Prefecture.

The *kiriha-zukuri* ("cutting-edge style"; pls. 30, 31) represents the first stage in attempts to solve this problem. Its flat side thinning to the edge made it possible for the smith to combine strength and efficiency in cutting. The problem was finally solved by the invention of the *shinogi-zukuri* ("ridge style"), in which the thickness of the metal decreases towards the back of the sword as well as towards the cutting edge. (These and other sword features mentioned in this text are illustrated in the Introduction, pls. 2–13.)

The curved sword of *shinogi-zukuri* type may have been perfected as late as the second half of the Heian period (eleventh and twelfth centuries) and was probably due to the smiths Sanjō Munechika in Kyoto, Yasutsuna of Hōki province, and Tomonari and his pupils of the Ko-Bizen school. The earliest dated sword of this type to be discovered so far is a *tachi* by Ki no Namihira Yukimasa dated 1159. Although the works of the three great smiths just mentioned are technically superior to and more elegant than Yukimasa's, his blade forms a useful basis for dating.

49

TACHI FROM THE HEIAN TO THE KAMAKURA PERIOD

The special features of *tachi* from the Heian to the Kamakura period may be summed up as follows.

(1) They are ridged, about 80 centimeters long, and rather narrow.

(2) They are strongly curved near the hilt (a feature called *koshizori*), mostly in the range of 2.7 to 3.0 centimeters measured as the greatest distance between the back of the blade and a line drawn from the tip to the point where the polished metal ends and the unpolished tang (*nakago*), the part that goes inside the hilt, begins.

(3) The width of the blade at the transverse ridge (*yokote*) near the point is 50 to 65 percent that of the blade at the section where the tang begins (the *motohaba*), and in relation to the *motohaba* the length of the point of the blade (the *kissaki*) measures 60 to 70 percent. This type of *kissaki*, relatively short in proportion to the width near the tang, is called *ko-kissaki* ("small *kissaki*"). Such blades predominate at this period probably because these *tachi* were used from horseback to stab the enemy's throat, making a long point—which was more useful for the sweeping, slashing strokes previously associated with cavalry warfare—unnecessary.

52

32. Detail from the *Heiji kassen emaki*, or "Heiji Insurrection Scroll." Color on paper. H. 42.3 cm. Kamakura period. Tokyo National Museum.

33. Rubbing (*oshigata*) of a *tantō* signed *Hisakuni*. *Nagasa* 20.3 cm. Blade early Kamakura period. Collection of Matsudaira Yorizane.

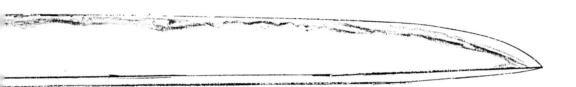

The *tachi* of this period were worn slung edge downwards from the waist (see pl. 32) and were accompanied by a small companion sword known as the *koshigatana* ("waist-knife"). This *koshigatana* was a short sword whose mounting included no guard (*tsuba*) fitted at the point where the tang of the blade enters the hilt; this style is known as *aikuchi* (literally, "fitting mouth"; the mouth of the scabbard meets the hilt directly without a guard intervening). Very few *koshigatana* survive from this period, but in the Itsukushima Shrine on the Inland Sea near Hiroshima there is an example decorated in mother-of-pearl with paulownia *mon* or badges, which is said to have belonged to the shogun Ashikaga Takauji (1305–68). The blade, signed *Tomonari*, is an example of the work of the Ko-Bizen school but unfortunately it has been damaged by fire at some time and subsequently retempered.

Other typical examples of swords dating from the early Kamakura period include a *tantō*, or short daggerlike blade, by Awataguchi Hisakuni (pl. 33), who is said to have been a member of the distinguished group of swordsmiths that waited on the retired Emperor Gotoba (1180–1239, r. 1183–98), and a *tantō* from the hand of Yukihira of Bungo province. The *tantō* by Hisakuni is in *hira-zukuri* form with no

53

34. Example of a *chōji hamon*.

35. Example of a *saka chōji hamon*.

ridge, the line of the back shows a slight curve towards, rather than away from, the edge (a feature called *uchizori*), and the temper-line is *komidare*, with small and frequent irregularities.

Among the swords of the early Kamakura period is a type known as *kodachi* ("small *tachi*") about whose original use there are a number of theories. According to one of these it served as a companion blade to the normal-sized *tachi*, while according to another it was designed for use by adolescent warriors. It is difficult to be sure which of these conjectures is correct. In the *Heike monogatari* and other collections of heroic tales written during the thirteenth century we sometimes read of warriors wearing "several swords" but it is not known exactly what is meant by this.

Kodachi are extant by Yoshikane of the Ko-Bizen school, Norishige of Etchū, and Sadazane of Yamato-Hōshō and, later in the Kamakura period, by Niji Kunitoshi and Rai Kunitoshi, both of Yamashiro province, as well as Mitsutada and Nagamitsu of the school centered at Osafune in Bizen province. It may perhaps be significant that the production of *kodachi* is confined to certain areas or schools and to a fixed period of time. The *kodachi* is in the normal *tachi* shape and is mounted in *tachi* style, but it is less than 60 centimeters in length.

THE MID-KAMAKURA PERIOD

As the *bakufu* (military, as opposed to imperial government) at Kamakura in eastern Japan became more securely established and a new and tangible *samurai* or warrior spirit began to emerge, the center of cultural activities shifted steadily from Kyoto to Kamakura. It was in the attempted Mongol invasions of 1274 and 1281 that the Japanese nation faced its greatest military crisis. In the first action it was saved by a great storm which sank the entire Mongol fleet. In preparation for a second invasion the *bakufu* sent edicts to every province ordering great efforts to be made to improve naval defenses and military capability. One of the results of these efforts was a magnificent new style of sword, the *ikubi-kissaki no tachi* (see pl. 60), with its great width and thickness at the ridge. The superb swords made around this time by Rai Kuniyuki, Niji Kunitoshi, Ichimonji Sukezane, Saburō Kunimune, Osafune Mitsutada, and others testify to the defiant spirit of the Japanese people during the crisis. Another important feature of swords produced at this date is the beautiful outline of the tempered edge, or *hamon*, known as *chōji* (see pls. 34, 35). Of the many theories

36. Reproduction of a detail from the *Mōko shūrai ekotoba*, or "Mongol Invasion Scroll," in the Imperial Household Collection. Color on paper. Original late thirteenth century. Tokyo National Museum.

concerning the origin of the term *chōji* I favor that which ascribes it to the similarity of the *hamon* pattern to the tightly packed buds of the *jinchōge* plant (*Daphne odora*; clove).

Around this time we suddenly begin to find large numbers of fine *tantō* being produced. This is probably due to the fact that, hitherto, swordsmiths had been less careful in the forging of *tantō* than of *tachi* because the short sword was not used in hand-to-hand single combat. When warriors began to place greater reliance on novel methods of close combat, often involving an element of surprise, swordsmiths began to concentrate their energies on the production of the *tantō*, which was more serviceable than the longer *tachi* in such encounters. In the famous *Mōko shūrai ekotoba*, a narrative scroll depicting one of the Mongol attacks (pl. 36), there is a scene in which a Japanese warrior who has boarded an enemy ship appears to have pinned down a Mongol general by attacking him from behind and is shown about to cut his head off with a *tantō*. This suggests that it was the problems posed by the unfamiliar threat of a seaborne invasion which led to the perfection of new fighting techniques.

Tantō of this period, as we have seen from the example of Hisakuni above, have no ridge, are mostly rather narrow, and are usually about 24 to 25 centimeters in length, with the line of the back curving slightly towards the edge. Around the beginning of the fourteenth century, *tantō* became slightly longer, about 27 to 30 centimeters, and as a result slightly wider, with either no curve at all or only a very slight *uchizori*.

Fine *tantō* survive by, among others, Tōshirō Yoshimitsu (pl. 37) of Yamashiro province, said to have been Kuniyoshi's pupil, and by Shintōgo Kunimitsu (pl. 38) of Sagami province, teacher of the great Masamune and Yukimitsu and founder of the Sagami tradition. Among the famous unsigned *tantō* of Masamune there are three called Hōchō Masamune ("Kitchen-Knife Masamune"; pls. 39, 67). They are about 22 centimeters long and 3.5 to 3.6 centimeters wide, and it is probably the slight curve towards the back which accounts for their nickname "Kitchen-Knife." One of the *tantō* of Norishige of Etchū, a pupil of Masamune (pl. 40), is unusual in that its combination of slight curve towards the cutting edge and very gentle tapering at the point makes it resemble a bamboo-shoot at first glance. This so-called *takenoko-zori* ("bamboo-shoot curve") of the blades by Norishige is useful in identifying his work. The Taima (or Tōma) and Shikkake schools of Yamato province, on the other hand, produced two types of *tantō*: one in the normal, flat *hira-zukuri* style and the other in a ridged style known as *kammuri-otoshi-zukuri* ("cap-slope style") in which the distance between back and ridge varies considerably.

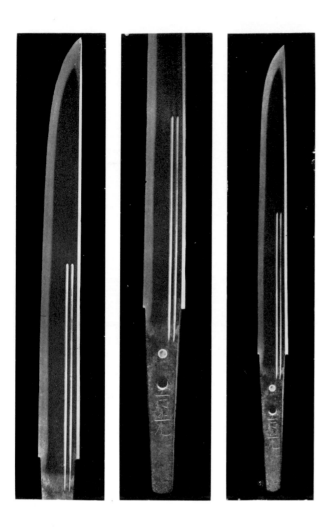

37. "Shinano Tōshirō." *Tantō.* Signed *Yoshimitsu.* Steel. *Nagasa* 25.2 cm. Thirteenth century. Collection of Sakai Tadaaki.

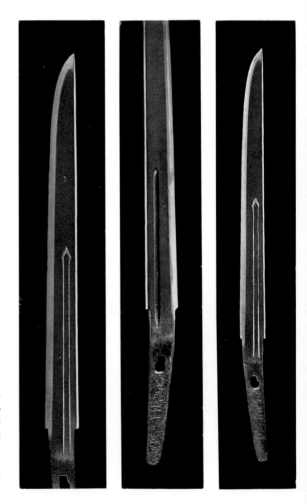

38. *Tantō.* Signed *Kamakura no jūnin Shintōgo Kunimitsu saku* ("Made by Shintōgo Kunimitsu of Kamakura"). Dated *Einin gannen jūgatsu mikka* ("The third day of the tenth month of the first year of Einin [1293]") on the reverse. *Nagasa* 23.5 cm. Thirteenth century. Collection of Miyazaki Tomijirō.

58

39. "Hōchō Masamune." *Tantō.* By Masamune. Steel. *Nagasa* 21.8 cm. Late Kamakura period. Eisei Bunko, Tokyo.

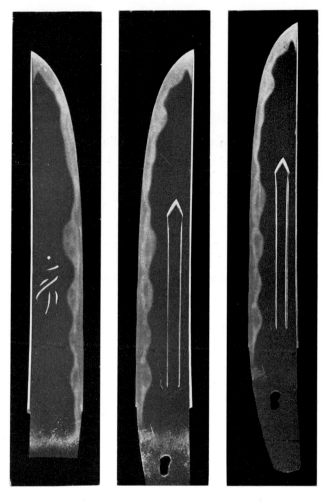

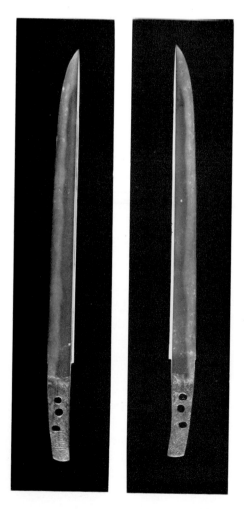

40. "Nippon'ichi." *Tantō.* Signed *Norishige.* Steel. *Nagasa* 24.5 cm. Late Kamakura period. Eisei Bunko, Tokyo.

59

From around the middle of the thirteenth century halberds (*naginata*) of fine quality began to be produced. In the *Hōgen monogatari*, *Heiji monogatari*, *Heike monogatari*, and other thirteenth century collections of tales of the twelfth century wars there are a number of incidents in which *naginata* are used, although no actual examples survive from the periods described. Probably they were regarded at the time as expendable weapons and were not therefore produced with great care. The situation changed, however, when they came to be made by such great masters as Nagamitsu and Kagemitsu of Bizen or Sukemitsu of the Yoshioka Ichimonji line. Of the *naginata* made in Yamashiro province the most famous is the so-called Honebami Tōshirō ("Bone-gnawing Tōshirō") ascribed to Tōshirō Yoshimitsu. This became an heirloom of the Ōtomo family of northern Kyushu and was called the Ōtomo *naginata*. It was presented at one point to the shogun Ashikaga Takauji but the blade was later returned to the Ōtomo family. When the great military dictator and unifier of Japan, Toyotomi Hideyoshi (1536–98), made his expedition to Kyushu in 1587 he was presented with the weapon by a member of the family. It escaped injury by fire at the fall of Osaka Castle (1615) when Hideyoshi's son Hideyori (1593–1615) was defeated by Tokugawa Ieyasu (1542–1616), the founder of the Tokugawa shogunate, and came eventually into the hands of Ieyasu's son Hidetada (1579–1632). Unfortunately, it was damaged during the great fire at Edo in 1657. It has now been retempered and is kept in the Toyokuni Shrine at Kyoto, which is dedicated to the memory of Hideyoshi. There are also extant a fine *naginata* by Rai Kunitoshi and an unsigned example of the work of the Taima school.

THE NAMBOKUCHŌ PERIOD

The swords of the Nambokuchō period (1333–91) represent the culmination of the tendency towards greater and greater length which began to manifest itself at the end of the Kamakura period. Naturally there are still *tachi* of normal size but, generally speaking, a length of from 90 to over a 100 centimeters became the norm. The short and narrow *tantō* disappears, giving way to a thick, wide, curved type of companion sword called *ōdabira* or *ōdanbira*. The *naginata*, which was widely used at the time, became longer, reaching 70 to 80 centimeters. There is no parallel for these ostentatious weapons in earlier periods; the most likely reason for their popularity at this time is the existence of two rival imperial courts which felt obliged to outdo one another in displays of military might. Such enormous weapons were not in fact necessary from a practical point of view. Some of the so-called *ōtachi* ("great *tachi*") were as much as 1.3 or 1.5 meters long; they are also known as *seoidachi* ("back-carried *tachi*") because they were borne into battle carried over the soldiers' shoulders rather than slung at the waist. It is recorded that when in actual use they were wrapped in cord down to the middle of the sharpened part but it is not clear what practical purpose was served by this measure. The larger *naginata* were popularly described as *nagamaki* ("with long wrappings"); this expression, however, applied not to the blade of the weapon but to the long strips of material which were wrapped round and round its handle. Both kinds of wrapping were probably used to enhance the ostentatious show of power which these weapons were intended to make.

During the Nambokuchō period a new type of *hamon* called *hitatsura* was used for the first time on swords produced in Sagami province. In the *hitatsura* style the marks left by the tempering appear in the area round the ridge as well as near the edge of the weapon. This style, in which isolated patches of tempered metal appear irregularly over the whole blade as well as in the *ha*, had a great influence on the later history of sword manufacture in Japan. Another characteristic *hamon* of this period is the *sakachōjimidare* of the Aoe school of Bitchū province in which the undulations of the temper-line are sharp and pronounced, forming wavelike protrusions which point towards the end of the blade. The *sakachōjimidare hamon* and others like it are indications of the current widespread popularity of variations on the basic, classical theme of *notare* (large, slow undulations) and *gunome* (sharp undulations).

THE MUROMACHI PERIOD

In 1392, at the end of the Nambokuchō period, the two rival courts were united, and in 1394 Ashikaga Yoshimochi (1386–1428) set up a government in the Muromachi district of Kyoto. The general peace which prevailed, briefly, at the beginning of the following Muromachi period had its effect on the development of the Japanese sword, since it meant that boastful ostentation was no longer necessary. The establishment of a new *bakufu* at Muromachi made people think of returning to the ways of the ancient Kamakura *bakufu*; *tachi* produced at this time recall in style the swords of the mid-Kamakura, with relatively narrow blades and points (*kissaki*) of only moderate length. There is, however, one important difference: these Muromachi-period blades are curved near the point (*sakizori*) rather than near the hilt (*koshizori*). This preference for *sakizori* can probably be attributed to the rise in popularity around this time of a new type of sword called the *uchigatana*, which differs from the *tachi* in being worn edge upwards in the belt.

The *uchigatana* developed out of the ever-increasing need for speed in combat, and its rapid acceptance is clear evidence of the degree to which fighting had become fiercer and more intense in early fifteenth century Japan. With the *tachi*, the two actions of drawing and striking are quite distinct; but with the *uchigatana*, because the sword is drawn from below, the action of drawing becomes the action of striking. For a soldier fighting on horseback, a *sakizori* curve is essential in such a blade, since it allows the sword to come out of the scabbard at the most convenient angle for striking an immediate blow. *Uchigatana*, whose mounts frequently include a guard, were forged in both long and short lengths. Those over 60 centimeters were called *katana* —which is the usual word for sword in modern Japanese—and the shorter blades 61

were called *wakizashi* ("companion sword"). The *uchigatana* illustrated in plate 41 is a typical example. Called the Akechi Koshirae (*koshirae* being the general term for a sword mounting) because it was used by Akechi Mitsuharu (d. 1582), the cousin of Nobunaga's turncoat general Mitsuhide, it is covered in plain, almost raw, black lacquer. The hilt is wrapped in green cord and there is a pierced iron guard.

The word *uchigatana* can be found in literary works as early as the Kamakura period, but at that time the blade was used only by people of low status and privates in the ranks. Most *uchigatana* produced at this early date were very roughly made and because they were regarded as disposable virtually no examples survive today. It was not until the Muromachi period, when generals and samurai began to use them to supplement their *tachi*, that *uchigatana* of high quality were made.

As we have said, *tachi* made at this date exhibit a return to the style of the Kamakura period, and we find the same tendency in *tantō*. Most of these are rather short and even the longer than average *tantō* are narrow in comparison to their length. There are some examples with no curve. Towards the end of the period a completely new type of *tantō*, only about 15 centimeters long, became popular. These extra-short *tantō* were probably carried secretly in clothing rather than worn at the waist. Another special characteristic of Muromachi-period *tantō* is the prevalence of the two-edged style, resembling the *tsurugi* of early times in having two cutting edges but differing from it in two respects: the ridge is not centrally placed and there is sometimes a slight curve. Many two-edged *tantō* were made by the later Bizen school of Sukesada, Katsumitsu, Munemitsu, and others, by the later Seki school of Mino province, and by the schools of Hiroga of Hōki province and Muramasa of Ise province.

It is often claimed that the Muromachi period was a kind of dark age in the history of the Japanese sword. Although it must be admitted that it was not distinguished by the emergence of successive generations of outstanding smiths (as was, for example, the late Kamakura), it was important for the large number of innovations which were made at the time. Because there are so many special characteristics to look out for, the whole Muromachi period presents a great challenge to the professional sword-appraiser.

41. "Akechi Koshirae." *Uchigatana* mounting. Steel. L. 87.7 cm. Muromachi period. Tokyo National Museum.

The *hamon* styles of the preceding period were maintained: this is in fact the peak period for the *notare* and *gunome* patterns, and the *hitatsura* is fashionable as well. Characteristic variants of the *gunome* are the *sambonsugi* (see the Introduction) of Kanemoto, the *gunome chōji* (combination of *gunome* and *chōji*) of Kanesada, the *fukuro gunome chōji* ("pouch *chōji*") of Kanefusa (all three of these smiths worked at Akasaka in Mino province), and the *kani no tsume* ("crab claw") of the Sukesada line in Bizen province. Other characteristic *hamon* styles of the period are the even and symmetrical *konotare* (*notare* with small undulations) and *gunome* of Muramasa and Heianjō Nagayoshi. These distinctive *hamon*, when considered in conjunction with that part of the tempered edge in the point of the blade called the *bōshi*, are extremely valuable guides in the assessment of Japanese swords.

This was a period in which use of lances (*yari*) and *naginata* was particularly widespread. The shape of the *naginata* was roughly as before, but the elongated point and the strong *sakizori* curve are especially noticeable. Muromachi-period *naginata* are not as large and imposing as in the Nambokuchō period but they give an impression of great sharpness and in the hands of determined and strong samurai they must have been highly effective weapons.

The *yari* is a new version of the Nara-period *hoko*, of which there is a wide variety of types in the Shōsō-in, all of them differing from the *yari* of the Muromachi and subsequent periods in that their tang is made hollow to receive the wood or bamboo handle, while the *yari* is more usually fitted with a long thin tang held inside the material of the handle by a peg (*mekugi*) in the same way as a normal sword. Some *yari* of Nara-period *hoko* form are found, but these are called *fukuro yari* ("bag *yari*") rather than *hoko* even if they are identical with Nara-period *hoko*. Of the large *yari* which became fashionable at the end of the Muromachi, the *ryōshinogi-zukuri* ("two-ridged form"), the *sankaku-zukuri* ("three-cornered form"), and the *sasaho-zukuri* (ridged in the center of one side only) all originated earlier in the same period. *Yari* were carried by squads of samurai on foot who would charge forward with the points of their weapons ranged in a row. They were also carried by men on horseback, among whom there existed a spirit of keen rivalry in the use of the new weapons.

42. "Nippongō." *Yari*. Steel. *Nagasa* 79.2 cm. Later Muromachi period. Kuroda Collection.

The well-known *yari* called the Nippongō (pl. 42) is 79 centimeters long, flat on one side and ridged on the other, with a design of Buddhist origin consisting of a dragon wrapped round a sword (*kurikara*) carved in a groove on the flat side. It is probably a work of the school of Kanabō of Yamato province. The Tombogiri ("Dragonfly Cutter"; pl. 43) is, like the Nippongō, one of the eminent "Three Spears of Japan" and was a favorite weapon of Honda Heihachirō Tadakatsu (1548–1610), a leading general of Tokugawa Ieyasu. Over 40 centimeters long, it is a large-scale weapon of the *sasaho-zukuri* type, and it bears the signature of a smith of Ise province called Fujiwara Masazane.

Spears were celebrated throughout subsequent history: at the battle of Shizugadake (1583), when Toyotomi Hideyoshi defeated Sakuma Morimasa (1554–83), seven of Hideyoshi's most valiant warriors used spears against the enemy. These men have been renowned ever since as the "Seven Famous Spearmen of Shizugadake." The spear used on this occasion by Katō Kiyomasa (1562–1611), one of Hideyoshi's principal lieutenants, was a large weapon almost 60 centimeters long made by one of the Sukesada of Bizen province. Another famous *yari* is the *katakamayari* (*yari* with sicklelike protrusions; pl. 44) used by the same Katō Kiyomasa in his campaign against Korea (1592). *Katakamayari* were widely used in the late sixteenth century and were effective both for striking and for stabbing.

The subject-matter of the carvings (*horimono*) on Muromachi-period blades is markedly different from that characteristic of the Heian and following periods. Carvings of the Buddhist deities Daikokuten, Bishamonten, and Marishiten appear for the first time, evidence that the samurai now revered them as war gods in addition to the traditional grouping of the Buddhist guardian deity Fudō, Hachiman, Amaterasu, and the god of Kasuga Shrine.

43. "Tombogiri." *Yari*. Steel. *Nagasa* 43.8 cm. Later Muromachi period. Collection of Yabe Toshio.

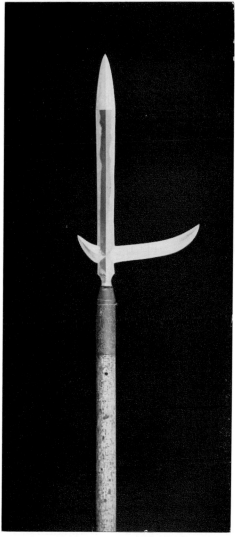

44. *Katakamayari* used by Katō Kiyomasa. Steel tip; shaft wood with mother-of-pearl. L. of tip 32.7 cm. Later sixteenth century. Tokyo National Museum.

The Momoyama and Edo Periods

The most important development in the late sixteenth century and early seventeenth century was the almost total abandonment of the *tachi* and the adoption of the custom of wearing a pair of long and short *uchigatana* together. Such a pair is called *daishō* (literally, "big-little"). We may never know exactly when the new style first appeared but in the Oyama Shrine, Kanazawa city, there is such a *daishō* once used by the powerful warlord Maeda Toshiie (1538–99; pls. 1, 54–55), with scabbards decorated in red and gold sprinkled lacquer (*makie*) which can be attributed to the Tenshō era (1573–92), as can the *daishō* with red-lacquer scabbards wrapped in gold foil given to another warlord, Mizoguchi Hidekatsu (1538–1600), by Toyotomi Hideyoshi (pl. 74), indicating that the custom of wearing two swords first became popular in the late sixteenth century. But these early *daishō* mounts differed from their successors in that they did not always have the characteristic metal fittings, in particular the matching large and small *tsuba*, and many of the blades used in them were old *tachi* which had been drastically shortened. This was common practice with *tachi* of the Kamakura and still more of the Nambokuchō period, and blades formed in this way had a very shallow curve especially suitable for use by soldiers on foot.

Swords of the Momoyama period and later are called *shintō* ("new swords") and many were modeled on these shortened and unsigned blades (the part with the signature having been cut away) of earlier periods. The resulting similarity of form is dramatically demonstrated if we compare one of these shortened swords with a *tachi* by Umetada Myōju, a leading smith of the period (pl. 45). This was not a case of copying for its own sake, since the new shape was ideal for the fighting technique of the time, which was chiefly on foot rather than on horseback. The development of *kendō*, formal training in swordsmanship, increased demand for the new type of sword.

It remains unexplained why the short *wakizashi* came to be used in addition to the long *katana*. From a formal point of view the practice of using the two together resembles the traditional association of *tachi* and *tantō* but, as we have already explained in connection with plate 36, the *tantō* has a practical function while there appears to be no convincing need for the use of the *wakizashi*. It is perhaps possible that the *katana* was a weapon of outdoor warfare while its companion blade was used for indoor fighting, a hypothesis which may be inferred from the fact that it was customary on entering a palace or castle to leave the *katana* on a rack in the entrance hall and proceed armed with *wakizashi* alone. It may be, therefore, that it was in order to be in readiness for combat both outdoors and indoors that the *daishō* pair was worn.

As a result of the adoption by the samurai class of the *daishō* as the formal style the *tantō* suffered a marked decline in use. Some of the longer *tantō* were of course mounted as companion swords in both the Shintō and Kotō periods but for the most part they were worn on their own at home by daimyo and higher-ranking samurai or else given

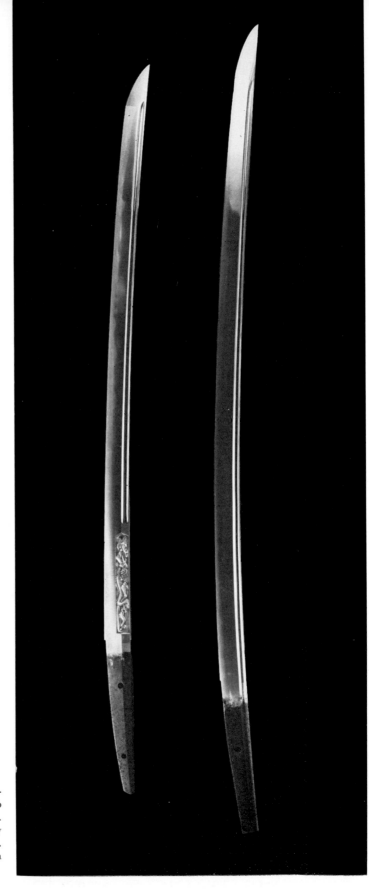

45. RIGHT: Greatly shortened *tachi* (converted to a *katana*). Unsigned; attributed to the Shizu school. Steel. *Nagasa* 73.6 cm. Nambokuchō period. LEFT: *Katana*. By Umetada Myōju. Steel. *Nagasa* 64.7 cm. Dated Keichō 3 (1598). Collection of Sōma Keiin.

unpleasant names such as *harakirigatana* ("belly-slitting sword") and used for ritual suicide. As there was an adequate supply of old *tantō* it was rarely necessary to have new ones made. *Yari* and *naginata* suffered a similar decline in the Shintō period. They were mainly used as ornamental pieces in daimyo processions (although *naginata* were sometimes also carried for self-defense by samurai women) and because only their shape mattered no care was necessary in their manufacture. As a result there are no really fine examples.

The most widespread and popular styles in the Shintō period were the Sagami, Bizen, and Mino traditions, with the Yamashiro and Yamato traditions playing a lesser role. In the early part of the period the best smiths working in the Sagami style were the Horikawa school led by Shinano-no-kami Kunihiro and the Echizen Shintō group surrounding Yasutsugu. Characteristics include the Sagami *itame* grain in the tempered edge, a wavy and spiral texture similar to wood grain; *nie*, which are minute particles of crystalline structure appearing like silver sand, in the area between the edge and the ridge (*nie* in this area are called *jinie*); the *notare hamon* with large *nie* and shiny areas of curved outline called *kinsuji*; and fine carvings, or *horimono*, which are well suited to the blade as a whole. For the most part the Sagami blades call to mind the work of Sadamune and Masamune but there are also pieces strongly influenced by the style of Ono Hankei of Edo, itself based on the style of Norishige, one of Masamune's pupils, and by the style of Nanki Shigekuni, itself based on the style of another of Masamune's pupils, Gō Yoshihiro.

In the mid-Edo period even pieces which differ in style from that of the Sagami masters mentioned above are said to be in Sagami style provided they have good, bright *nie*. The late eighteenth century connoisseur Kamada Gyōmyō, who published books on Shintō (1777) and Kotō (1796) swords, praised even the highly unorthodox *hamon* of Tsuta Echizen-no-kami Sukehiro called *tōran midare*, or "billow *midare*," as a marvel in the Sagami tradition. Kamada also called the smith Inoue Shinkai "the Masamune of Osaka." Shinkai's swords have a very compact *koitame* grain with large *jinie* and *chikei* (shining areas of curved outline in the main body of the sword). His *hamon* is a very slightly undulating *suguha*, as opposed to true *suguha*, which is absolutely straight. Shinkai's swords also exhibit many *nie* and *nioi*, with extensive *kinsuji* in the edge. Shinkai's style is comparable to that of Yukimitsu of Sagami province. The work of the Edo smith Nagasone Kotetsu strongly resembles that of Gō Yoshihiro, the pupil of Masamune mentioned above. On his swords the metal of both the area between the tempered edge and the ridge (the *ji*) and of the edge itself is outstandingly bright and clear.

During the Momoyama and early Edo periods the smiths of the Ishidō school specialized in the Bizen style; the individual smiths of the line are hard to identify. Many of their blades have in the past been mistaken for masterpieces of the Kotō period whose signatures have been lost through being filed away or through shortening of the blade. The school split into four principal groups during the mid-Edo period: the Osaka Ishidō group of Kawachi-no-kami Kunisuke II (called Naka-kawachi), Tsuta Sukehiro mentioned above (nicknamed Soboro), Tatara Nagayuki, and others; the Edo line, consisting of the successive generations of the Ishidō Sakon Korekazu name, Hioki Mitsuhira, and others; the Kii province line of Bitchū-no-kami Yasuhiro, Kawachi-no-daijō Yasunaga, and others; and the Chikuzen province line of which Moritsugu and Koretsugu are outstanding representatives. These Ishidō swords have the *chōji* edge, while the surface of the blade between the *hamon* and the ridge exhibits unusually tinted patches of metal which form an exact reflection of the *hamon*. This effect is known as *utsuri* ("reflections"). The swords of the Ishidō school include pieces which approach in excellence the work of the masters of the Ichimonji and Bizen Osafune schools of the Kamakura period.

The school of Tadayoshi of Hizen province in Kyushu was skillful both in the straight *hamon* (*suguha*) reminiscent of Rai Kunimitsu of Yamashiro province (four-teenth century) and in the irregularly undulating *midare* style. Among the practitioners of the Yamato tradition there are Yamashiro-no-daijō Kunikane, protégé of the warlord Date Masamune of Sendai (1567–1636); his successors, who followed the thirteenth and fourteenth century Hōshō school and produced pieces rivaling the old masters; and, in Kii province, Shigekuni, protégé of the daimyo Tokugawa Yorinobu of Wakayama (1602–71), who forged successfully in the manner of his ancestors of the Tekai Kanenaga line of Nara. Another imitator, in the mid-Edo period, of the *suguha* and the straight wood-grain texture called *masame* of the Hōshō school was Ogasawara Nagamune.

The Mino tradition was carried on throughout the country as a result of the dis-persal of the Seki smiths from their traditional center during the fifteenth and sixteenth centuries. Most of their swords are mass-produced pieces of no real quality, but in the Shintō period we find, among the works of the various smiths who moved to such provinces as Yamashiro, Owari, Kaga, and Echizen, many pieces of fine make which perpetuate the old Mino techniques. Mino-style smiths include, in Kyoto, Iga-no-kami Kimmichi, Tamba-no-kami Yoshimichi, Etchū-no-kami Masatoshi of the Mishina school (pl. 46); in Kaga province Kanewaka (pl. 47), protégé of the Maeda family; in Owari province Sagami-no-kami Masatsune, Hida-no-kami Ujifusa, Hōki-no-kami Nobutaka, and others; and in Echizen province Kanenori, Kanesaki, and others. These smiths naturally copied the works of the Nambokuchō period, the golden age of the Mino sword, but the style of the Muromachi period was followed by Tashiro Kanemoto, Kanenobu, and other Edo-period smiths who worked at Seki, the old center of the Mino school, while Darani Katsukuni in Kaga province forged blades with the *sambonsugi hamon* of Kanemoto and the style of Kanemoto's great contemporary, Kanesada, was preserved by the succession of smiths called Kanesada who worked in Imazu, Mutsu province.

The great antiquarian revival of the late Edo period, which advocated a return to purely Japanese rather than Chinese and Buddhist cultural values, wrought a   71

46. *Katana.* Signed *Etchū no kami Masatoshi* ("Masatoshi, governor of Etchū province"). Steel. *Nagasa* 77.5 cm. Early seventeenth century. Collection of Taguchi Ginosuke.

powerful change on the world of the swordsmith. Earlier Edo styles were modified and it became fashionable to copy closely the swords of the Kamakura and Nambokuchō periods. The leading exponent of this new tendency was Kawabe Gihachirō Suishinshi Masahide (d. 1825), who worked for the Akimoto family of Yamagata, and his theories were put into practice by Shōji Daikei Naotane. The revivalist vogue immediately caught on throughout Japan and over a hundred smiths began to follow Masahide's teachings. At first they copied the *tōran midare* invented by Tsuta Sukehiro, but as the new way of thinking took hold it was the old Sagami and Bizen styles which were most influential. The Bizen copies were particularly successful.

Minamoto Kiyomaro, an outstanding smith of this Shinshintō ("New-New Sword") period, was dissatisfied with the tradition established by Masahide and made a special study of the Sagami subtradition called Shizu from the name of the place in Mino province where Saburō Kaneuji, another Masamune pupil, lived. Kiyomaro made successful copies in this style, of which the characteristic features are a *hamon* combining *gunome* and *notare* with irregular *nie* and lines of *nie* (*sunagashi*) in the edge. Having decided on a career as a swordsmith Kiyomaro moved to Iga-chō in Yotsuya, Edo, and became known as "the Masamune of Yotsuya." Other skilled imitators of the Sagami tradition were Yamato-no-kami Motohira and Hōki-no-kami Masayuki of Satsuma province. Some of their swords have had their signatures removed and later been mistaken for genuine old Sagami blades of the highest quality. In the Shinshintō period the Yamato tradition, which had been kept alive by the Kunikane smiths of Sendai mentioned above, was also copied by Katsumura Norikatsu of Mito and his many pupils. They produced swords with *suguha* and the brilliant *masame* grain which was also used by Kiyomaro's pupil Kiyondo.

MODERN SWORDS

In 1876, eight years after the restoration of the Meiji Emperor, an edict was promulgated forbidding the samurai to wear swords, and the smiths lost their means of livelihood. Later, after the Sino-Japanese and Russo-Japanese wars (1894–95 and 1904–5), there was a fresh appreciation of the true value of the Japanese sword and blades began to be forged again, mainly for use as swords for officers in the national army. These are called *gendaitō* ("modern swords"). In the meantime most smiths had

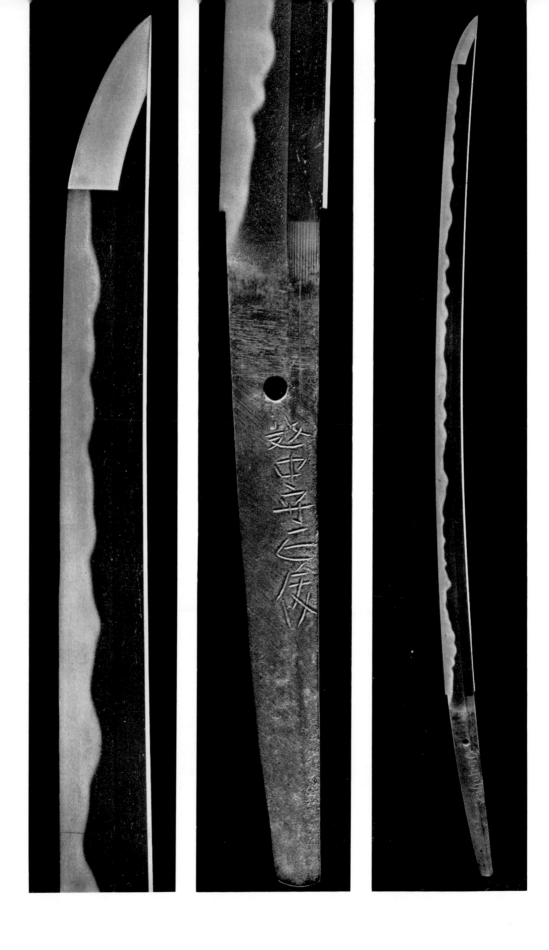

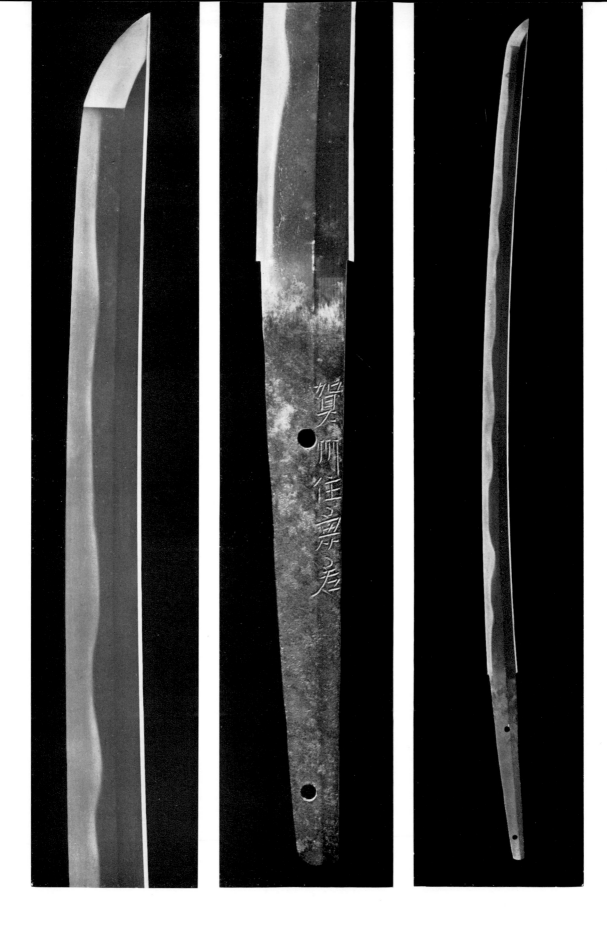

47. *Katana*. Signed *Kashū no jū Kanewaka* ("Kanewaka of Kaga province"). Steel. *Nagasa* 69.7 cm. Early seventeenth century. Collection of Taguchi Ginosuke.

abandoned sword making but one man, Gassan Sadakazu of Osaka, kept the craft alive. In 1906 he was appointed a Craftsman to the Imperial Household and until his death in 1919 at the age of eighty-four he devoted himself to forging swords. Although he was best in the Bizen style he was an extremely versatile smith who was equally at home with the Sagami, Yamashiro, and Yamato traditions. His *horimono*, too, are very fine, especially his dragons, *hatahoko* (banners topped by a lancehead), and Fudō deities. Another Craftsman to the Imperial Household was Miyamoto Kanenori, pupil of Yokoyama Sukekane of Okayama in Bizen. He worked as a swordsmith for about sixty years until his death in 1926 at the age of ninety-seven, but he was far inferior in skill to Sadakazu and few of his blades survive today although they played an important role as blades for officers' swords. During World War II the heavy demand for such swords was met not only by true smiths but also by makers of agricultural implements who switched to sword production. Since the swords of this period were made by smiths who lacked proper training and were in any case intended only for use by army officers, no fine blades were produced.

Japan's defeat in the war dealt a second major blow to the world of the sword. The manufacture of weapons of any kind was strictly forbidden by the Western occupying forces and swords were of course included in the ban. The 1876 edict had only applied to the wearing of swords rather than to their manufacture and its effect was less devastating. However, in 1953 a new law was introduced which included the provision that there was no obstacle to the forging of swords provided permission had been previously obtained from the Committee for the Protection of Cultural Properties. In 1954 the Society for the Preservation of Japanese Art Swords held the first postwar exhibition of craft swords, and since then there have been many more such events.

Even before this, in 1949, when about sixty swords were required for the important renewal ceremony at the Ise Grand Shrine, an event which has taken place at roughly twenty-year intervals for over a thousand years, the occupying forces had granted permission for their production. These were not curved swords of the typical Japanese kind but archaic blades in *kiriha* style; the longest ones measured from 80 to 96 centimeters. Ten smiths were selected for the task of making these swords. Bearing in mind the absolute dedication of the swordsmith to his calling we may well imagine the joy felt by those who were chosen for this opportunity to practice their craft again

48. *Katana*. By Takahashi Sadatsugu. Steel. *Nagasa* 33.0 cm. Dated 1960. Private collection.

and the disappointment of those who were passed over. The shrine renewal ceremony went off without a hitch, and among the smiths who presented swords were such men as Miyaguchi Toshihiro, Takahashi Sadatsugu (pl. 48) and Miyairi Akihira (pl. 49), who are now both designated as preservers of Important Intangible Cultural Assets (popularly known as Living National Treasures), and others such as Ishii Akifusa, Nigara Kunitoshi, Endō Mitsuoki, and Sakai Shigemasa. A number of other items, *hoko*, *tōsu*, and arrowheads, were presented at the ceremony and these too were manufactured by the specially chosen smiths. All in all, the 1949 ceremony was the first important stimulus given to the swordsmiths of Japan in the postwar period.

Before the war modern swords were a kind of post-Edo-period continuation of the Shinshintō tradition and usually no more than a second-class version. Because they were largely intended as blades for officers' swords, collectors and connoisseurs before the war did not show much interest in new swords; they were mostly regarded as utilitarian artifacts and it was only very rarely that they were treated as art objects worthy of aesthetic appreciation. After the war the sword enjoyed a revival of interest both as a work of art in steel and as an expression of the Japanese spirit. As a result of this new interest in the aesthetics of the sword people were no longer satisfied with the second-rate prewar blades. Under the leadership of the Society for the Preservation of Japanese Art Swords a number of smiths have striven to produce swords of the quality demanded by the postwar generation of collectors. This has necessitated a return to basic principles: first of all the prewar style had to be abandoned, and instead of relying exclusively on the finest industrial carbon steel, smiths had to mix it with scraps of old iron so that each could create his own peculiar material which would in the process of forging bring life and activity to the surface of the blade. It was also necessary to study tempering methods, the shaping of the tang, and other details such as the correct way to engrave signatures.

The ten years or so after the war saw the abandonment of the officers' sword style of the Meiji, Taishō, and early Shōwa eras and the birth of the first blades to take their inspiration from the masterpieces of the Kotō period. Efforts to live up to the Kotō ideal have continued. Since there is no limit to the heights of quality to which an ambitious artist-craftsman can aspire, one can expect that these efforts will continue in the future.

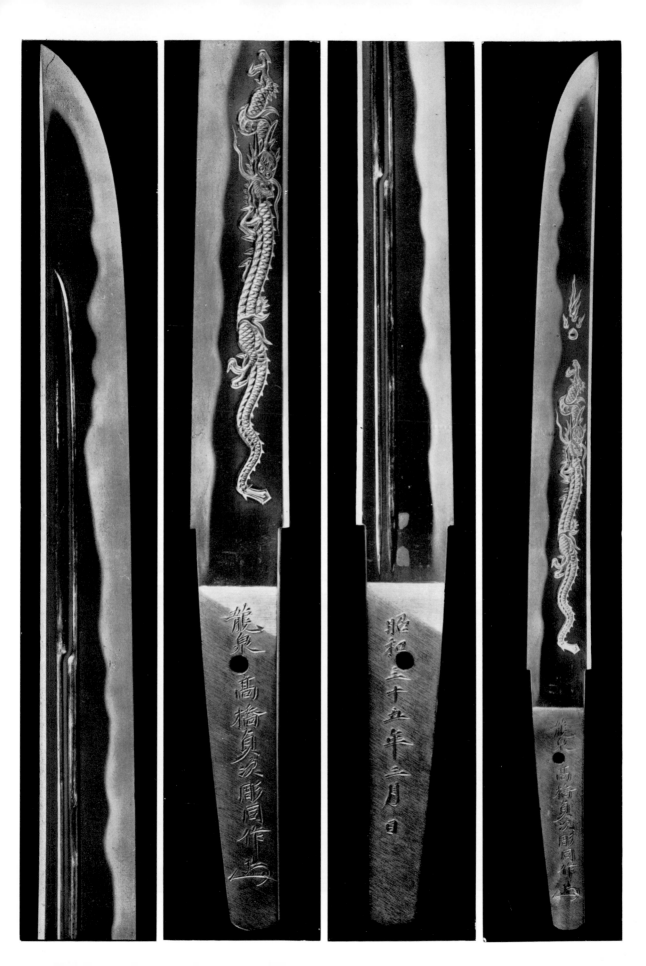

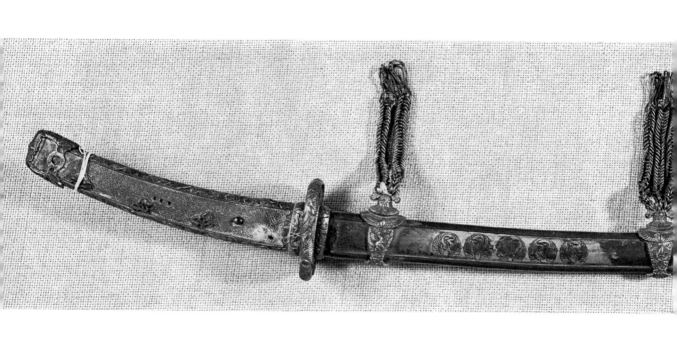

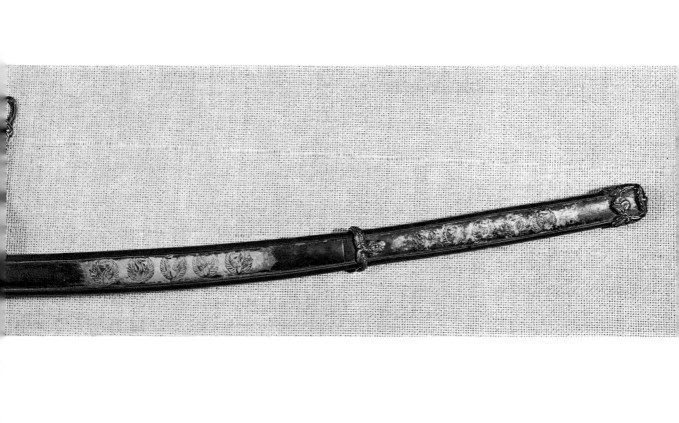

52. *Sasamaru* mounting for a *tachi*. Scabbard and guard covered in black-lacquered leather; upper part of scabbard and hilt wrapped with silk bands. L. 106.0 cm. Nambokuchō period. Atago Shrine, Kyoto.

This severely practical mounting is said to have been worn by Ashikaga Takauji (1305–58). The leather bag covering the leather guard is designed to protect it from damp; the wrapping of the upper part of the scabbard guards it against damage from rubbing against armor when slung from the warrior's waist.

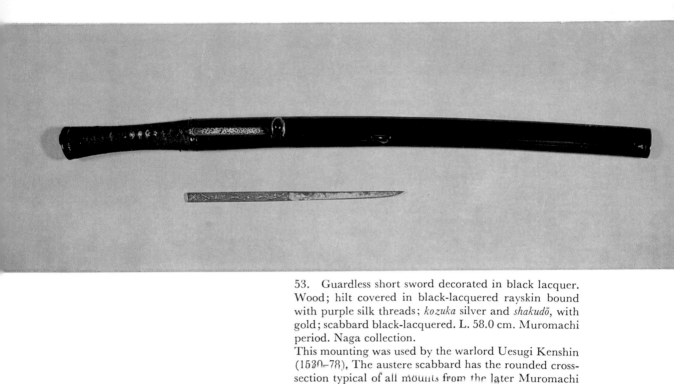

53. Guardless short sword decorated in black lacquer. Wood; hilt covered in black-lacquered rayskin bound with purple silk threads; *kozuka* silver and *shakudō*, with gold; scabbard black-lacquered. L. 58.0 cm. Muromachi period. Naga collection.

This mounting was used by the warlord Uesugi Kenshin (1530–78). The austere scabbard has the rounded cross-section typical of all mounts from the later Muromachi period onwards. There are two *kozuka*, small knives, one on either side of the hilt, an unusual feature. We would normally expect either a *kozuka* on one side only or a *kozuka* on one side and a *kōgai* (skewer) on the other side.

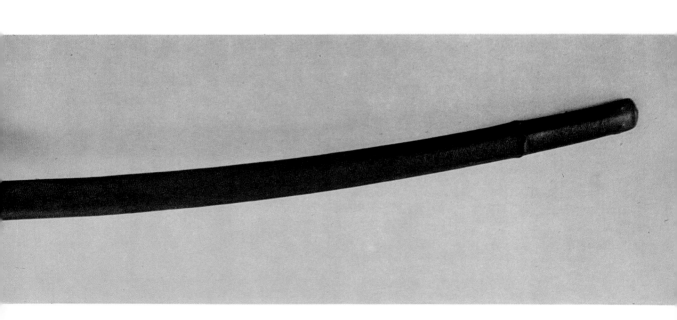

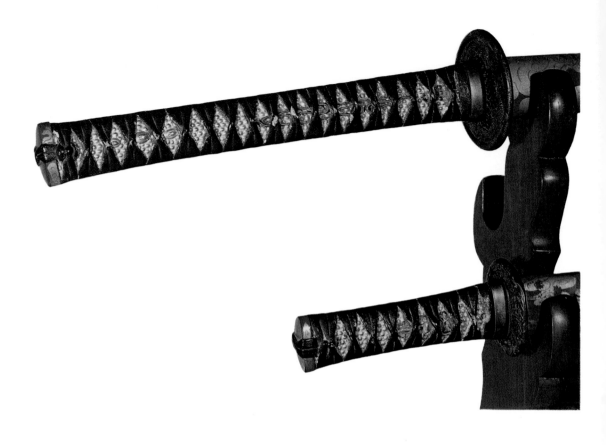

54–55.   Details of *daishō* mounting in plate 1. Oyama Shrine, Ishikawa Prefecture.

This pair of long and short swords was worn by Maeda Toshiie (1538–99), a leading figure in the wars of the Momoyama period, and is one of the finest and best-preserved examples of the Momoyama *daishō*. The extreme length of the *katana*, the exaggerated proportional length and waisted form of the hilts, and the lacquered rayskin are typical features of these early *daishō* mountings. The austere iron guards offset the extravagant effect of the rest of the ensemble and thus exemplify the combination of display and restraint that characterizes warlord taste in this period.

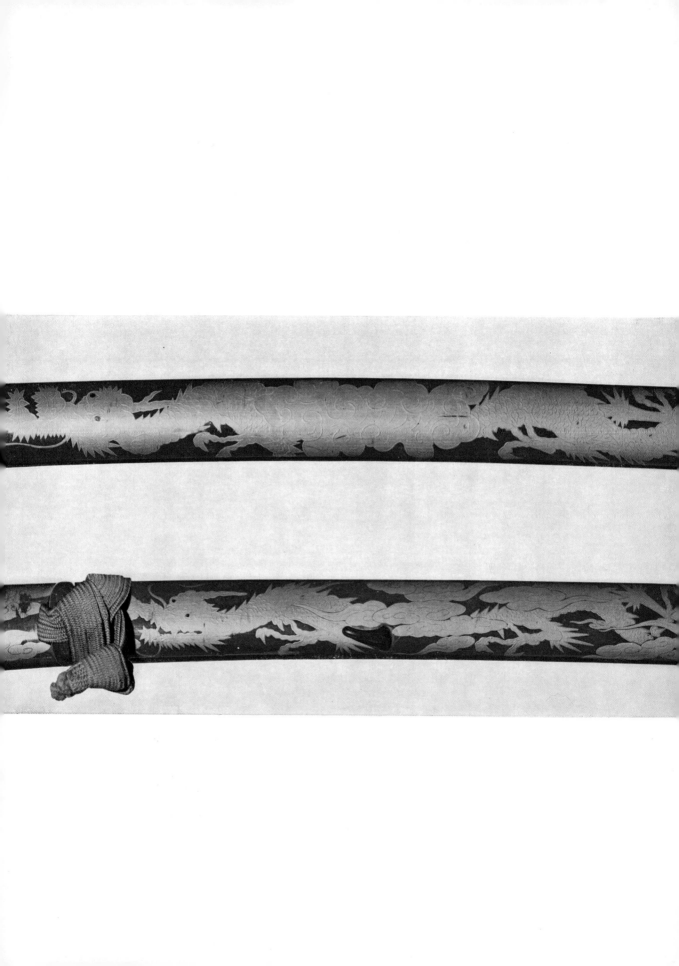

56. RIGHT: Short sword mounting with peony designs. Copper, with carved and gilded metal fittings and semi-precious stones. L. 43.2 cm. LEFT: Short sword mounting with fish and net designs. Wood with decoration in *yamagane* (a dark impure copper). L. 42.7 cm. Early Muromachi period. Tokyo National Museum.

Elaborately decorated short swords (*koshigatana*) like these were in widespread use from the Kamakura period to the end of the Muromachi period and were worn in conjunction with *tachi*. The left-hand sword is said to have been owned by the warlord Kimura Shigenari (1593–1615).

2

THE APPRECIATION OF FINE SWORDS

The finest swords are known in Japanese as *meitō* (literally, "swords with a name" or "famous swords"), but the absence of a signature on a blade does not necessarily preclude its being a *meitō*. There are more important considerations. To qualify as a *meitō* a blade must have a good shape, appropriate to its function as *katana* or *tachi*; it must be well constructed, be strongly and finely forged, and have an accurate temper-line. All the special features of its school and period must be visible at first glance, yet it must have an individual character of its own. The tang must be just as it was at the time of manufacture (such a tang is described as *ubu*). If a tang has been cut down we may say that "this is a *meitō*, but the state of the tang is to be regretted"; if the tang on a *tachi* is unaltered but also unsigned we may say, "if only there was a signature this could be called a *meitō*." In both cases, although the sword is in essence a *meitō*, conditions have to be attached.

There is a further condition to be borne in mind when assessing the status of a sword: only if it has been well known since the time of its manufacture is it a *meitō*. Hence it is impossible for any new *meitō* to be discovered by chance. For a sword to be famous throughout its life it must of course have a history. This historical background, especially if it involves associations with famous men and events, adds a great deal to a sword's status and value and plays a very important part in its proper assessment.

This is not to say, however, that a sword can be a *meitō* merely by virtue of its historic associations. There is a sharp contrast here with some other areas of Japanese craft. If a teabowl is known to have been used by a great man or admired by famous teamasters, this in itself is enough to make it a valuable object. A great sword, on the other hand, must combine superlative quality and an illustrious history. No matter how exalted its previous owners or how stirring the events it has witnessed, a sword cannot be a *meitō* if it is a forgery or inferior in technical quality. A true connoisseur would have nothing to do with such a pretentious artifact. A *meitō* must appear to be a *meitō* whoever sees it, but there are cases of swords which have been accorded *meitō* status in error, due to lack of sufficient expertise or to mistaken reliance on mere financial value.

In 1719 the Hon'ami family, hereditary sword-appraisers to the Tokugawa sho-gunate, were ordered by the eighth shogun, Yoshimune (1684–1751), to make a written appraisal of all the *meitō* in Japan. The result was the *Kyōhō meibutsuchō* (Catalog of Famous Things), and each sword listed in the book came to be known as a *meibutsu* ("famous thing"). All the *meitō* in the possession of the shogun and daimyo are listed but, Tōshirō Yoshimitsu apart, there is a rather excessive emphasis on the Sagami tradition of Masamune and Gō Yoshihiro at the expense of the Bizen smiths. Yoshimitsu, Masamune, and Yoshihiro are popularly revered as the three greatest smiths of all time. Yoshimitsu was known above all as a maker of fine *tantō*, and his works were said to possess a spirit which protected their owners, so that many daimyo houses handed them down as family treasures. Masamune is regarded as the greatest representative of the Japanese sword in general and his best pupil, Gō Yoshihiro, is especially regarded because his works are very scarce. The popular acclamation of these three smiths as the best of all time should not, however, be taken as an absolutely unchallengeable assessment.

At one time it was said that no *meibutsu*, be it teabowl, painting, or sword, was ever of sure quality, and this criticism has been applied to the swords in the Hon'ami *Meibutsuchō* on the grounds that the Hon'ami compilers had no real freedom of opinion, expression, or choice since they were subservient to their feudal masters. It is argued that as a result the *Meibutsuchō* includes many swords which lack the necessary high quality or have dubious signatures or other features. Critics of the *Meibutsuchō* also point to its inclusion of blades which exhibit a variety of faults: some have been heavily polished down or show signs of general wear while on others the hard steel surface is breaking up or the edge is damaged. But defects of this type could, in fact, have come about after the blades in question were examined by the Hon'ami appraisers. In fact there is a section in the *Meibutsuchō* devoted to "lost blades," famous swords of the past which were destroyed or damaged by fire on such occasions as the fall of Osaka Castle in 1615 or the great fire of Edo in 1657. These are, of course, no longer *meitō*, but they were included out of regard for a great sword's associations. Some of those listed were blades which had been rescued and subsequently retempered, but the section also includes blades known to have been destroyed without trace and those whose whereabouts were unknown. Leaving these lost or damaged blades aside and bearing in mind the occasional lapses resulting from the social constraints on the Hon'ami, we find that the majority of the swords in the *Meibutsuchō* are indeed fully worthy of the name *meitō*.

It should be mentioned that there are some *meitō* which are not included in the *Meibutsuchō*. These are swords which were given special names and kept secretly by certain daimyo houses either because they had a particularly close connection with the history of the family in question or because they were especially treasured.

The rest of this chapter will be devoted to an appraisal of some *meitō* which are representative of the various stages in the history of the Japanese sword.

57. "Dōjigiri." *Tachi*. By Yasutsuna. Steel. *Nagasa* 80.0 cm. Mid-Heian period. Cultural Properties Commission.

BLADE: curve 2.7 cm. *Shinogi-zukuri, fumbari*, strong *koshizori, iorimune, ko-kissaki*.

GRAIN: *koitame*, with many *jinie* visible in the metal as *utsuri* in the edge.

HAMON: *komidare*, with many *ashi* and *konie* and here and there brightly shining *kinsuji*.

BŌSHI: *komaru*, with well-defined and strong *hakikake*.

TANG: *ubu*. Signed *Yasutsuna* in two characters carved above the *mekugiana*, the character *yasu* slightly to the left of the ridge and *tsuna* somewhat more central.

TACHI, BY YASUTSUNA

This *tachi* is a masterpiece which sums up the achievements of the smiths of the mid-Heian period and brings to mind the grace and elegance of the culture of that epoch (pl. 57). In feeling it is resolute and refined, rather than crude and savage; the edge is in the *yakiotoshi* style, typical of the tempering of a number of early blades, in which the tempered edge starts a little above the *hamachi* rather than from the area of the upper tang just below the *hamachi*, which is the notch separating the blade proper from the tang on the sharp side of the blade. The earliest examples of swords with this feature are in the Shōsō-in, Nara. Yukihira, a smith who worked in Bungo province in the latter part of the Kamakura period, is particularly noted for his use of *yakiotoshi*, and it is commonly seen in early works by smiths from Kyushu as well as in swords of the Ko-Bizen school and occasionally in those of the Bizen school of the Kamakura period. When seen on a sword it is often a sign that retempering has taken place, but one should not jump to the conclusion that this is always so. Also worth mentioning here is that the position of the characters forming the signature is a consistent and notable feature of Yasutsuna's blades.

According to old sword books, Yasutsuna lived in the Daidō and Kōnin eras (806–23) in Hōki province, but since his swords are close in style to works by other smiths who are known to have worked in the second half of the Heian period (i.e., from about 1000 onwards) and very different from those in the Shōsō-in, this traditional dating cannot be accepted. The tradition that Yasutsuna was a resident of Hōki province is supported by the evidence of the signatures on the blades of Sanemori, said to be his son, which read, "Sanemori of Ohara in Hōki." The link between the two smiths is further established by the marked mutual resemblance of their works. The name Dōjigiri ("Dōji Cutter") was first used in the Muromachi period and is recorded in the Hon'ami *Meibutsuchō*, according to which the blade is so called because it was used at Mount Ōyama by Minamoto no Yorimitsu (also called Raikō, 948–1021) to slay the Shutendōji, a brigand with magical powers. There may well be some historical incident on which this tradition is based.

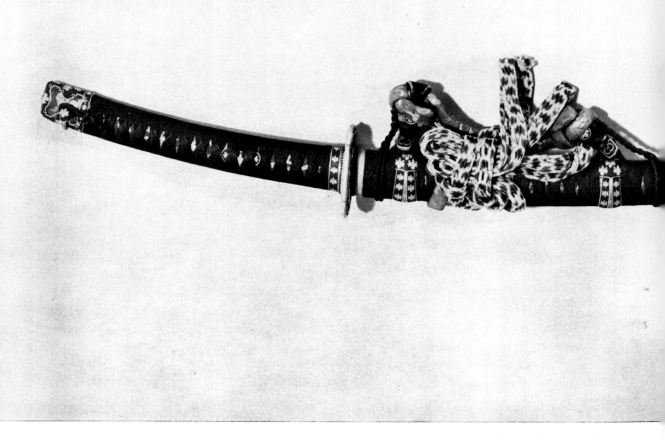

58. *Itomaki no tachi* mounting with paulownia and chrysanthemum badge decoration. Scabbard wood decorated in gold *nashiji* and *hiramakie* ("flat" *makie*) and partially wrapped with silk bands; hilt wood covered in silk brocade wrapped with silk bands; metal fittings *shakudō* and gold. L. approx. 120.0 cm. Momoyama or early Edo period. Private collection.

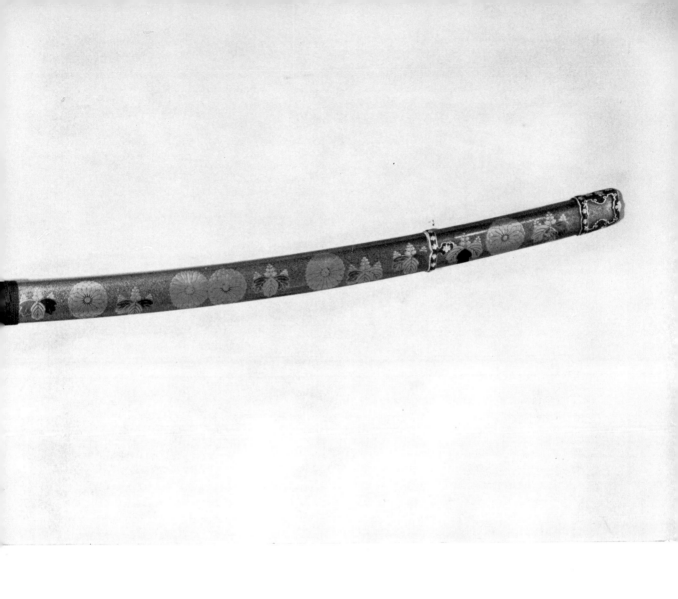

The Dōjigiri was presented to Oda Nobunaga, the leading late sixteenth century general (1534–82), by the Ashikaga family; subsequently it was the property, in turn, of Toyotomi Hideyoshi and Tokugawa Ieyasu. The second Tokugawa shogun, Hidetada, bestowed it on the daimyo Matsudaira Tadanao (1595–1650) of Echizen, but after the disgrace and dispossession of the Echizen Matsudaira occasioned by some irregular conduct on the part of Tadanao, the blade passed to the Tsuyama branch of the family.

The present mounts of the Dōjigiri (not illustrated here) are fine examples of Momoyama-period work in *itomaki no tachi* style, in which the typical wrapping of the hilt continues along part of the scabbard (pl. 58). The scabbard is decorated in gold *nashiji* (gold flakes suspended in transparent lacquer) and the metal fittings are of *shakudō* (a blue-black alloy of copper with a small percentage of gold) worked with a *nanako* (granulated) ground and bearing the imperial paulownia *mon* (family badge or crest) in gilt.

This is undoubtedly the finest of the few blades by Yasutsuna which survive today. It is perhaps the most celebrated of all Japanese swords.

93

59. "Ō-Kanehira." *Tachi*. By Kanehira. Steel. *Nagasa* 89.2 cm. Mid-Heian period. Tokyo National Museum.

BLADE: curve 3.4 cm., *motohaba* 3.7 cm., *sakihaba* 2.5 cm. *Shinogi-zukuri*, pronounced *fumbari*, strong *koshizori*, *iori-mune*, *chū-kissaki*.

GRAIN: compact *koitame* with *midare utsuri*.

HAMON: *midare*, with many *ashi*, *konie*, and *nioi*, and a few *kinsuji*.

BŌSHI: continues the *midare* outline of main blade, but for part of the length the temper-line is double.

TANG: *ubu*. *Sujikai* filemarks sloping sharply to the right. Signed *Bizen no kuni Kanehira* ("Kanehira of Bizen province").

TACHI, BY KANEHIRA

The maker of this fine and imposing blade was, as the signature indicates, Kanehira of Bizen province (pl. 59). He was a swordsmith of the Ko-Bizen school, and his great reputation rests especially on this one magnificent blade whose metal and edge are as clear and beautiful today as they were at the time of manufacture. The great width of the blade is probably intended to draw attention away from its length. On each side is a broad and skillfully carved groove ending in a point (*kakinagashi*) just below the *munamachi*, the indentation between the ridge and the tang, opposite the *hamachi*. These grooves add an indefinable quality to the blade as a whole. The signature on the outside of the blade, which is the side that faces away from the wearer's body when the *tachi* is slung edge downwards from the belt, is in thick, confident strokes.

The Ō-Kanehira and the Dōjigiri have traditionally been regarded as the finest of all *meitō*. Which of the two we put first is really a matter of subjective taste rather than objective expertise. The Ō-Kanehira takes the lead in terms of sheer magnificence and splendor, but it cannot match the Dōjigiri in quiet and classical elegance.

Kanehira and his two contemporaries of the Ko-Bizen school, Sukehira and Takahira, are known as the *sampira* ("three *hira*") of Bizen. A few of Sukehira's works survive, but no sword signed by Takahira or definitely his work has been found. A good many swords signed *Kanehira* do still exist, however; they are mostly narrow, with *ko-kissaki*, in the style typical of all Bizen *tachi* of the late Heian, and the signature is of two characters only (i.e., only the smith's name, without reference to his place of residence or to other information such as date). The blade presently under discussion differs from other signed Kanehira swords in several respects. The *kissaki* is of medium size in proportion to its width (*chū-kissaki*) rather than *ko-kissaki*, the blade is broader and longer, and in general the quality is higher, especially in the grain and the tempering. The signature was executed with a thicker than usual chisel and is larger than is normal for Kanehira. Probably it was the masterpiece of a lifetime and its strength and confidence fully justify the name Ō-Kanehira. The prefix *ō-* ("great") is quite commonly used in the names of blades, as in Ō-Mihara, Ō-Aoe, Ō-Kanemitsu, Ō-Tenta, Ō-Hōshō, and Ō-Kurikara Hiromitsu, usually with

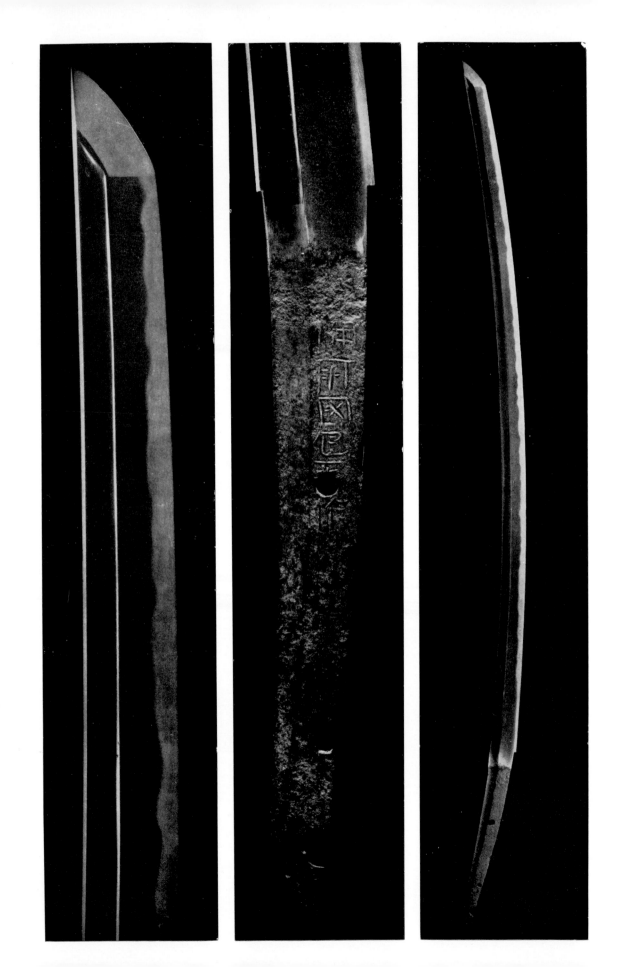

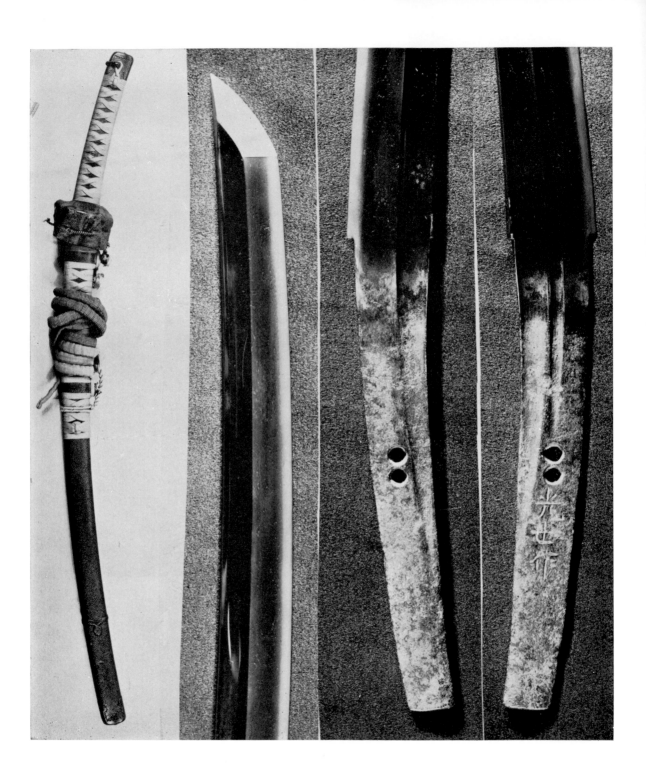

60. "Ō-Tenta." *Tachi*. By Mitsuyo. Steel. *Nagasa* 66.1 cm. Eleventh century. Maeda Ikutokukai, Tokyo.

BLADE: curve 2.7 cm., *motohaba* 3.5 cm. *Shinogi-zukuri*, *fumbari*, strong *koshizori*, *marumune*, *ikubi-kissaki*.

GRAIN: *nagare itame* with whitish *utsuri*.

HAMON: *hososuguha*, with small *nie* and a few scattered *ashi*.

BŌSHI: mostly straight, ending in a *komaru* turnback.

TANG: *ubu*. Signed *Mitsuyo saku* in center, below the *mekugiana*.

reference to size (in the case of the Hiromitsu, the size of the *kurikara horimono* is meant) but also as an acknowledgment that the sword is in each case the masterpiece of the smith who forged it.

By the time the *Kyōhō meibutsuchō*, in which it is listed, was compiled, the Ō-Kanehira was renowned throughout Japan and was already in the possession of the Ikeda family of Bizen province. The previous history of the Ō-Kanehira is uncertain, but there is a tradition that it was bought by the famous daimyo and lover of learning Ikeda Mitsumasa (1609–82), and it is said that at the time of its acquisition Mitsumasa was rebuked by the Confucian scholar Kumazawa Banzan (1619–91), who told his master that he should be using his money to attract the best possible advisers rather than squandering it on swords. Mitsumasa ignored him and bought the blade. However, according to the Ikeda family records, the Ō-Kanehira was a favorite blade of Mitsumasa's grandfather, Terumasa (1564–1613), one of Nobunaga's leading generals and a great sword-lover. In the *Meibutsuchō* alone several of his swords are listed, including the Ikeda Kunimitsu (a *tantō*), the Ikeda Masamune (a *katana*), and the Ikeda Sadamune (a *wakizashi*), and the Ō-Kanehira was no doubt one of his greatest treasures. The blade had a Momoyama-period *itomaki no tachi* mounting but this was unfortunately lost in the confusion following the war.

That the widely contrasting narrow Yasutsuna and broad, splendid Kanehira were both produced in the late Heian period should not be a matter for surprise, but it is true that there are very few surviving examples of the Kanehira type. Apart from the blade discussed here only the Ō-Tenta Mitsuyo (described in the next section), the Ko-Bizen Sadatsuna in the Kunōzan Tōshōgū shrine dedicated to Tokugawa Ieyasu in Shizuoka Prefecture, and a few others are known.

TACHI, BY MITSUYO

This blade, with its *motohaba* of 3.5 centimeters, is broad in proportion to its length (pl. 60). The metal is thick, and the forging is typical of the smith. At the edge of the *hamon* appears the brushed effect called *hotsure*, and for a length of 30 centimeters from the point towards the center of the blade, in the important striking part called the *monouchi*, the temper line is double, with exceptionally small *nie*. The tang lacks the normal taper, and on each side of the blade there is a wide, shallow, round-bottomed groove, or *bōhi*, tapering into the tang from the blade (*kakinagashi*). A short groove, or *koshihi*, extending halfway down the tang, is added on the outside. The signature, in three characters, has been done with a thickish chisel.

Mitsuyo lived in Miike, Chikugo province, Kyushu, and was usually called Tenta. After his retirement he is said to have taken the name Genshin. His signed works are very few. There is a *tachi* formerly in the collection of the Iwasaki family which has the same signature but was unfortunately retempered. Its present location is unknown. According to the old sword books there are swords signed *Tenta* and *Genshin* but I have never seen one with a Genshin signature, and although I have come across what appeared to be a Kamakura-period blade with the Tenta signature, further examination would be necessary to establish its connection with the present smith.

Ō-Tenta has been treasured since the time of Ashikaga Takauji. During the Muromachi period it was handed down in the shogunal family and, together with the Dōjigiri of Yasutsuna, the Mikazuki Munechika, the Ichigo Hitofuri Yoshimitsu, and the Juzu-maru Tsunetsugu, was one of the "Five Great Swords." The fourteenth Ashikaga shogun, Yoshiaki (1537–97), presented it to Hideyoshi, who in turn presented it to Maeda Toshiie, and it became one of the most treasured possessions of the Maeda family. It was closely guarded in a chest together with a small *tachi* by Munechika and a *naginata* of the Shizu school, and all three treasures were handled once a year only, by the head of the family. A tradition relates that because of the spirit of the Ō-Tenta birds were afraid to alight on the roof of the storehouse in which the chest was kept.

The mounting of the sword is in a leather-wrapped style called *onimaru-koshirae*, which was in widespread military use from the beginning of the Muromachi period. According to the *Kyōhō meibutsuchō* the *onimaru-koshirae* of the Ō-Tenta was made on the orders of the craftsman and sword expert Hon'ami Kōho (1601–82) in the time of Maeda Toshitsune (1593–1658).

Mention should also be made here of the Miike no Tachi, another sword by Tenta in the Kunōzan Tōshōgū. It is a little longer than the Ō-Tenta but all other features are the same in both swords, except that the tang of the Miike no Tachi, although it is *ubu*, is in *kijimomo* shape, narrowing sharply on the edge side, with a *kurijiri* butt.

Such was the faith of Ieyasu in the spiritual power of the Miike no Tachi that when, on his deathbed, he was still concerned about the unrest in the Kansai (the western part of central Honshu), he ordered that the sword be placed with its point towards that region in order to preserve the peace. It is still deep in the shrine at Kunōzan, where Ieyasu was temporarily buried on his death. Both *tachi*, the Ō-Tenta and the Miike, are the best available evidence on the swords of Kyushu in the Heian period.

TACHI, BY NORIMUNE

This relatively narrow sword (pl. 61) resembles the Heian-period pieces already discussed. The signature, in two characters, has been fluently inscribed with a fine chisel. Norimune was the founder of the Fukuoka Ichimonji school. He lived at Fukuoka in Bizen province (not to be confused with the modern city of the same name in northern Kyushu) and together with his son Sukemune was a member of the group of smiths who made swords for the exiled emperor Gotoba. The blade discussed here is the best of the very few works of Norimune which survive today. The forging is exceptionally fine, the tang is still *ubu* (always an important feature), and the sword as a whole is very powerful in form. The works of the Ichimonji school during this period closely resemble those of other schools, for example the Ko-Bizen, but there are slightly more *chōji* and *chōji utsuri*.

Norimune is often called Kiku Ichimonji ("Chrysanthemum" Ichimonji) because permission to use the imperial chrysanthemum *mon* was bestowed on him by Gotoba as a reward for his services, and he is said to have engraved the *mon* on his tangs. But since none of his surviving signed works have a *mon* on them the story may perhaps be doubted. It is recorded in the *Jōkyūki*, a historical work of the Muromachi period, and other sources that blades forged by Gotoba himself were carved with chrysanthemum *mon* having from sixteen to twenty-four petals and were called *kiku saku* or *kiku no gosaku* ("chrysanthemum make" or "imperial chrysanthemum make"). A number of such blades survive.

Blades also exist which are engraved with a chrysanthemum badge and, below it, the character *ichi*, consisting of a single horizontal stroke and meaning "one," from which the Ichimonji ("*ichi* character") school got its name. But such blades have no connection with Norimune and date from after the mid-Kamakura period. It is important to note that not only Norimune but also other smiths who worked for the imperial household were awarded the privilege of using the chrysanthemum *mon*. There is, for example, a *tachi* by Sukeshige of Bizen in the Meiji Shrine which has a sixteen-petaled chrysanthemum just below where the *habaki* metal collar fits at the beginning of the tang, and the *mon* is also found on a *tachi* by the mid-Kamakura-period smith Yoshihira, formerly in the possession of the Shimazu family, and on a blade by Unshō of Bizen, formerly in the possession of the Uesugi family. The Unshō sword may perhaps be accounted for by the fact that he worked for the emperor Godaigo (r. 1318–39), or it may be that the badge was added because the sword was for imperial use. To give another example, there is a *katana* by Izumi-no-kami Kanesada of the Mino Seki school which has on its tang a chrysanthemum which is not a false later addition. Since Mino province was originally an imperial domain the Mino smiths often worked for the imperial household and there is no reason why their blades should not have had the *mon* carved on them.

In the Shintō period there were many smiths who engraved the chrysanthemum *mon* and sometimes added the character *ichi* after it. The most famous of these is Kunikiyo (pl. 62), a pupil of Horikawa Kunihiro who after his master's death in 1614 returned to his native province of Shinano and soon afterwards entered the

61. *Tachi*. By Norimune. Steel. *Nagasa* 78.4 cm. Late Heian or early Kamakura period. Hie Shrine, Tokyo.

BLADE: curve 2.8 cm., *motohaba* 2.6 cm., *sakihaba* 1.6 cm. *Shinogi-zukuri*, *fumbari*, strong *koshizori*, *iorimune*.

GRAIN: tight *koitame* with *midare utsuri*.

HAMON: combination of *komidare* and *kochōji* ("small *chōji*") with active *ashi* and *yō* and, in places, *kinsuji*.

BŌSHI: slightly *midarekomi*; *komaru*.

TANG: *ubu*, in *kijimomo* shape with a narrow butt and slight curve. Signed *Norimune* just above the *mekugiana*, partially covering the ridge of the blade.

62. *Tachi*. Signed *Yamashiro no kami Fujiwara Kunikiyo* ("Fujiwara Kunikiyo of Yamashiro province"). Steel. *Nagasa* 74.2 cm. Early sixteenth century. Collection of Ise Torahiko.

63. *Tachi.* By Kuniyuki. Steel. *Nagasa* 69.6 cm. Late thirteenth century. Collection of Terada Koshirō.

BLADE: curve 2.7 cm., *motohaba* 2.1 cm. *Shinogi-zukuri, fumbari, koshizori, iorimune,* slightly *ikubi-kissaki.*

GRAIN: *koitame,* with many *jinie* and tempered areas in the *mune* (called *muneyaki*).

HAMON: almost *suguha,* but in places exhibits a combination of shallow *ōnotare, komidare,* and *chōji.* Rich in *nioi,* with many *ashi* and *yō.*

BŌSHI: *komaru.*

TANG: *ubu. Kiri* filemarks. Signed *Kuniyuki* below the *mekugiana.*

service of the Matsudaira family of Echigo province. In 1623, when Matsudaira Tadamasa (1597–1645) moved to Fukui in Echizen province, Kunikiyo followed him and became smith to the Echizen Matsudaira. In 1664 he received the honorary title Yamashiro-no-daijō ("Lord of Yamashiro province") and at the same time the use of the chrysanthemum *mon* was bestowed upon him by the imperial court, so that he came to be known as Kiku Kunikiyo, a name which was used by four or five successive generations, all of whom carved the *mon,* followed by the character *ichi,* on their swords.

It was originally thought that the first Kunikiyo instituted the custom of engraving the *ichi,* but as a result of subsequent research it appears that it started with the second generation. The sword illustrated in plate 62 is by Kunikiyo I and it has the *mon* without the *ichi.* Other smiths who made a regular habit of engraving the *mon* alone include Izumi-no-kami Kunitora and Hioki Echizen-no-kami Munehiro, while Echizen-no-kami Nobuyoshi and his school engraved the *mon* and the *ichi.* Care should be taken to avoid confusing their work with that of the Kiku Ichimonji school. There are a number of pieces of inferior quality in which the name of the smith has been removed, leaving only the *mon* and *ichi.*

TACHI, BY KUNIYUKI

In form and construction this is a fine sword (pl. 63). It is long in proportion to its width, and the *koshizori* and *fumbari* give the blade a balanced appearance. The use of *muneyaki* is typical of the Rai school, as is the *komaru* style in the *bōshi.* The evenly distributed *konie* are particularly beautiful; the metal and the edge are bright. *Kakinagashi* grooves taper into the tang on both sides.

Kuniyuki was the true founder of the famous Rai line of Yamashiro province which produced, in the mid-Kamakura period and later, such illustrious smiths as Niji Kunitoshi, Rai Kunitoshi, Rai Kunimitsu, and Rai Kunitsugu. No dated works of Kuniyuki are known, but there is a *tachi* by Niji Kunitoshi, dated Kōan 1, equivalent to 1278, and with this as a basis the approximate dates of Kuniyuki's activity can be estimated.

It has already been explained that, for the most part, *tachi* up to the mid-Kamakura were narrow and very elegant. About this time, however, we note the emergence of a

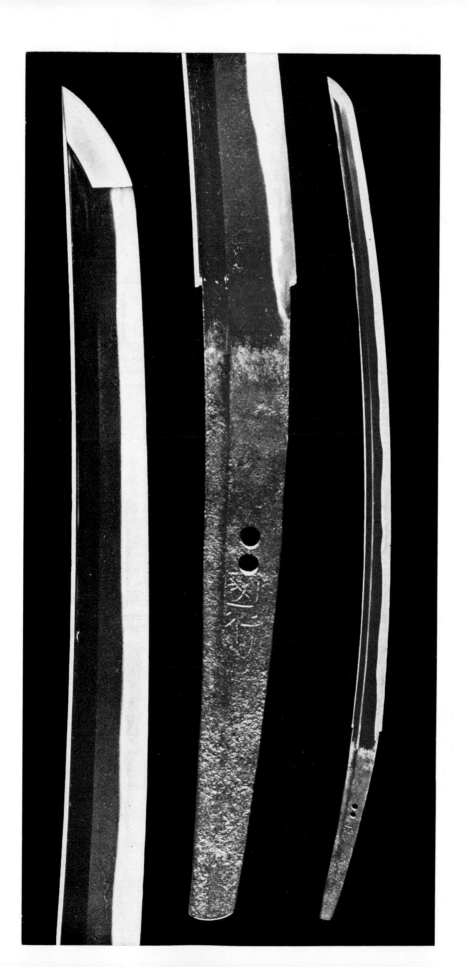

103

64. "Hirano Tōshirō." *Tantō*. By Yoshimitsu. Steel. *Nagasa* 30.2 cm. Late thirteenth century. Imperial Household Collection.

BLADE: Negligible *uchizori*, motohaba 2.9 cm. *Hira-zukuri, mitsumune*.

GRAIN: very tight *koitame*.

HAMON: *gunome* on both sides in the area of the *habaki-moto*; *chū-suguha* along the rest of the blade with slight *kogunome* and *konotare*. Dense, bright *nioi* and thick, clear *nie*.

BŌSHI: slightly turned back on both sides, *komaru* on one side and *togari* (pointed) on the other. Slight *hakikake* appearance at the edge.

TANG: *ubu*. Signed *Yoshimitsu* below the single *mekugiana*.

new style of *tachi*, more solid and imposing than its predecessors. This is a reflection of the change in taste which had come about as a result of the move of the capital from Kyoto to Kamakura. Kyoto was no longer the cultural center of Japan, and as the warrior class gained the ascendancy there was a transition in many of the arts to a stronger and more rugged style. The two attempted Mongol invasions in 1274 and 1281 also stimulated a change in *tachi* style: they encouraged the martial spirit of the samurai and made the development of weapons a matter of urgency. A new type of Japanese sword was necessary to cut through the strong armor of the Mongol troops.

The style of the signatures on the many surviving signed works of Kuniyuki is by no means consistent and there is evidence of a series of changes. The classic example here shows Kuniyuki at his powerful best.

TANTŌ, BY YOSHIMITSU

This is a large and broad *tantō* (pl. 64). Its very tight *koitame* texture verges on *nashiji*, a fine grain resembling the cut surface of a pear (*nashi*). There are active *ashi* right along the entire blade, and the *bōshi* is very skillfully executed. On both sides there is a groove set towards the back of the blade, and near the *habakimoto* the remains of an extra, narrow groove are visible. The signature has been engraved in large characters with a narrow chisel.

This *tantō* is listed in the *Kyōhō meibutsuchō*, which explains that it is called Hirano Tōshirō because it belonged to Hirano Michiyuki, a townsman of Settsu, from whom it was bought by Kimura Hitachi-no-suke for thirty-two gold *mai*. (Tōshirō is Yoshimitsu's personal name.) The *Meibutsuchō* goes on to tell us that at the time of its purchase it was a full *shaku* (approx. 30 cm.) in length, just as it is today. Thirty-two *mai*, equivalent to 320 silver *ryō*, was an enormous sum, but considering the peerless perfection of the blade, it was a gift at the price.

Kimura Hitachi-no-suke presented the blade to Hideyoshi who gave it to Maeda Toshiie. It was then presented to Tokugawa Hidetada, the second Tokugawa shogun, and in 1617 Hidetada returned it to Toshiie's son Toshimitsu at the time of his visit to the Maeda domains. On the same occasion the Maeda family presented Hidetada with another famous sword by Yoshimitsu, the Arami Tōshirō. Such formal exchanges were typical among daimyo families and it often happened that the most splendid

65. *Naginata.* By Ki no Sukemitsu. Steel. *Nagasa* 56.5 cm. 1320–21. Collection of Taguchi Ginosuke.

BLADE: curve 2.6 cm. *motohaba* 3.3 cm. *Unokubi-zukuri* ("cormorant-head shape"), *sakizori, mitsumune* near the tang and *iorimune* towards the point.

GRAIN: tight *koitame* with frequent *midare utsuri.*

HAMON: *kochōji* with *gunome.* Compact and bright *nioi* with occasional *ashi* and *yō.*

BŌSHI: *ōmaru.*

TANG: *ubu.* Signed *Ichi* and *Bishū Yoshioka no jū sakon shōgen Ki no Sukemitsu* ("Sakon-shōgen Ki no Sukemitsu of Yoshioka in Bizen province") on one side. Dated *Gen'ō ninen kinoe jūichigatsu* ("Gen'ō second year, eleventh month [1320–21]") on the reverse.

gifts presented at one meeting were returned at the next. The Hirano Tōshirō remained in the Maeda family until the Meiji period, but in 1882 it was presented to the Meiji Emperor.

The maker of this blade, Tōshirō Yoshimitsu, was a member of the mid-Kamakura-period Awataguchi school at Kyoto and is traditionally said to have been the son of Awataguchi Kuniyoshi. *Tantō* were undoubtedly his forte but *tsurugi* by him exist and there are a very few *tachi.* One, which has been called the Ichigo Hitofuri since early times, was one of the "Five Great Swords" mentioned above and was owned by successive shoguns during the Muromachi period. The name Ichigo Hitofuri, which was widely used during the period, means "once in a lifetime." This *tachi,* too, was presented to Hideyoshi, who had it cut down and fitted with a *gakumei,* that is, a signature removed from a blade when it is shortened and then fitted into the newly created tang. After that it was unfortunately damaged by fire at the fall of Osaka Castle, but Echizen Yasutsugu retempered it and it was handed down in the Owari branch of the Tokugawa family until it was presented to the Meiji Emperor. It also is now in the imperial household. At first glance it does not look as though it has been retempered and it remains, therefore, a beautiful piece of work.

NAGINATA, BY KI NO SUKEMITSU

The broadening of the point and the *sakizori* are typical features, making this a classic example of the calm and restrained *naginata* of the period (pl. 65). The features of the metal are particularly active in the lower part of the tempered edge near the tang, while the upper part is relatively plain. On both sides there is a main groove and a supplementary groove.

Literary sources provide evidence of widespread use of the *naginata* from the late Heian period onwards but the surviving examples are all mid-Kamakura or later. This is a representative Kamakura-period piece, important because of the flawless quality of its workmanship and because it has been handed down without alteration. It was originally an heirloom of the Maeda family. The Yoshioka Ichimonji school resided at Yoshioka in Bizen. Its original founder is not known but pieces inscribed with the words "resident at Yoshioka" are first found in the late Kamakura and carry on into the Nambokuchō period.

Tantō, by Kunimitsu

Kunimitsu, usually called Shintōgo, was the son of Kunitsuna, who moved from Awataguchi in Kyoto to Kamakura and was himself a pupil of Kunimune, who made the original move from Bizen province. Kunimitsu specialized in *tantō* but there are a few *tachi* surviving. He was the supreme master of the *suguha hamon*, which is first found on the early swords in the Shōsō-in and appears on swords made at all dates down to the present day. There were only a few smiths who were truly skillful in the production of *suguha* and of these Kunimitsu is undoubtedly the best. However, his work is often difficult to identify since old sword books tell us that he had three sons, Kunimitsu, Kunishige, and Kunihiro, all of whom signed their blades *Kunimitsu*. It is hard to distinguish the work of the four smiths accurately.

The blade Aizu Shintōgo (pl. 66) is large by comparison with Kunimitsu's other *tantō* and although early sources state that he was especially proficient in the production of the narrow *ito suguha* ("thread" *suguha*), this *tantō* has a broad *suguha*, suggesting that they were mistaken in their identification of his forte. The name of this magnificent blade, which is listed in the *Kyōhō meibutsuchō*, derives from the fact it belonged to Gamō Ujisato (1556–95), the wealthy lord of Aizu. It subsequently left the Gamō family and was bought by Maeda Toshitsune for a large sum, but in 1702 it was presented to the shogun Tsunayoshi (1646–1709) during his visit to the Maeda domains. Thereafter it remained the property of the shogunal house.

66. "Aizu Shintōgo." *Tantō*. By Kunimitsu. Steel. *Nagasa* 25.5 cm. Late thirteenth century. Collection of Aoyama Takayoshi.

BLADE: Negligible *uchizori*; *motohaba* 2.4 cm. *Hira-zukuri, mitsumune*.

GRAIN: extremely compact *koitame*, with frequent *chikei*.

HAMON: *suguha*, narrow near the tang and broadening towards the point. Very active edge, rich in *konie* and *kinsuji*.

BŌSHI: exceptionally fine *komaru* turning back very sharply at the point.

TANG: *ubu*, with *kurijiri* butt. *Kiri* filemarks. Signed *Kunimitsu* in center, beneath the *mekugiana*.

Tantō, by Masamune

This unsigned blade by Masamune, broad in proportion to its length and extremely thin, derives its name from its "kitchen-knife" (*hōchō*) shape (pl. 67). Two parallel grooves pass right through the blade and are embellished at their lower end with a clawlike engraving.

Masamune, perhaps the most famous of all smiths, lived at Kamakura in Sagami province, was a pupil of Shintōgo Kunimitsu, and was subsequently adopted by Yukimitsu, his predecessor in the Sagami school of smiths. The distinguished scholar and statesman Ichijō Kanera (1402–81) in his miscellany entitled *Sekiso ōrai* described Masamune as one of the great men of modern times and praised him as a smith whose blades were equal in quality to the sharp weapons of the Buddhist guardian deity Fudō himself. But because his signed works are exceedingly rare a theory was developed at the end of the nineteenth century that Masamune never existed at all. There is, however, ample evidence, both literary and derived from the swords themselves, to refute this notion. In the sword books of the Muromachi period the scarcity of signed blades by Masamune is accounted for by the explanation that his work was so absolutely distinctive that there was no need for a signature, but it is more likely that the reason lies in the fact that Masamune was a servant of the Kamakura *bakufu*. Many of his swords were made for shogunal use and it would have been presumptuous and contrary to all normal practice for him to have signed them.

109

67. "Hōchō Masamune." *Tantō*. By Masamune. Steel. *Nagasa* 21.6 cm. Late Kamakura period. Collection of Okano Katsuno.

BLADE: curve 0.3 cm., *motohaba* 3.8 cm. *Hira-zukuri, maru-mune.*

GRAIN: compact *itame* with many *jinie, chikei,* and *utsuri.*

HAMON: combination of leisurely *notare* and *mimigata* ("ear shape") with rich overall *nioi, konie,* and *kinsuji.*

BŌSHI: *midarekomi,* pointed turnback on front and rounded on other side, with *kinsuji.*

TANG: *ubu. Funagata* broadening towards the blade, with pointed *kengyō* butt. Incised with *sujikai* filemarks. Unsigned.

As we have indicated earlier, the appraisal of Japanese swords is a very difficult matter. The swords of Sagami province are the most difficult of all and years of accumulated experience are required before they can be accurately classified. Since it was particularly difficult during the feudal period to gain access to Masamune's blades a variety of erroneous theories and traditions concerning his work came into being.

The Hōchō Masamune is recorded in the *Meibutsuchō.* There are two other Masamune daggers which bear a marked resemblance to it, and in order to distinguish it from these other two it is sometimes called the Hōchō Sukashi ("pierced") Masamune, because of its two parallel pierced carvings. It was formerly an heirloom of the Naitō family of Nobeoka in Hyūga province, Kyushu. Of the other two, one was handed down in the Matsudaira Shimōsa-no-kami family of Oshi in Musashi province and has a Buddhist *ken* (straight sword) engraved on one side and *bonji,* stylized Sanskrit letters symbolizing Buddhist deities, on the other. At one time it was the property of Ankokuji Ekei (d. 1600), a Buddhist monk who was a trusted advisor of Hideyoshi. It is designated a National Treasure and is now kept by the Hosokawa family. The third sword, once an heirloom of the Owari Tokugawa family, is now kept by the Tokugawa Reimeikai in Nagoya. It is the largest of the three and is pierced with a *ken* shape. All three blades are unsigned but they share a number of stylistic features, in particular rich *jinie* and *chikei* in the *ji,* which are a common characteristic of all the best Sagami blades. Masamune's *hamon* is usually a refined, leisurely, and unfussy *notare* which other smiths have had the greatest difficulty in attaining. Added to this is the supreme quality of its embellishment with superb *nie, kinsuji,* and *inazuma,* a special type of *kinsuji* looking like lightning in clouds.

Traditionally, sword appraisers describe Masamune's *nie* as if they were bare patches in partially melted snow. They intend to convey by this expression the extremely varied character of his *nie* which could have been a fault in smiths of lesser quality but which for him became a point of excellence. Almost all Masamune's signed works are *tantō,* among them the Fudō Masamune, the Daikoku Masamune, the Honshō Masamune, and the *tantō* kept by the Kyōgoku family. Most of these blades have two-character signatures, but the Daikoku Masamune has a three-character signature *Masamune saku* ("Made by Masamune").

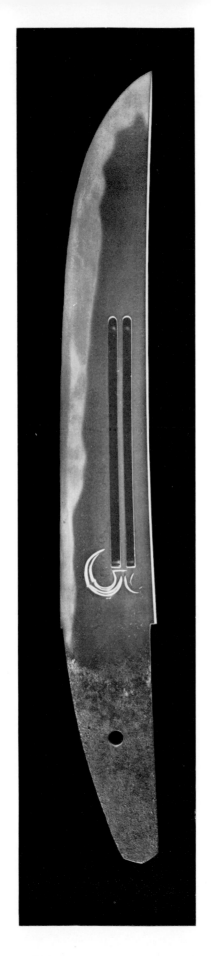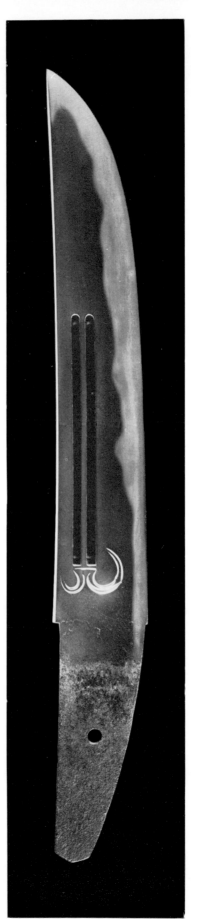

111

68. *Tantō.* By Sa. Steel. *Nagasa* 23.6 cm. Early Nambokuchō period. Collection of Aoyama Takayoshi.

BLADE: curve 0.1 cm., *motohaba* 2.3 cm. *Hira-zukuri, mitsumune.*

GRAIN: extremely tight *koitame* with narrow and dense *jinie.*

HAMON: *konotare* and *gunome* with deep *nioi* and thick and bright *konie.*

BŌSHI: sharp forward thrust with a long turnback.

TANG: *ubu.* *Ōsujikai* filemarks. Signed *Sa* below lower *mekugiana* on one side. Inscribed *Chikushū no jū* ("Resident in Chikushū") on the reverse.

TANTŌ, BY SA

This small blade has an almost imperceptible curve (pl. 68). The *bōshi* is typical of the smith, and the signature *Sa* has been confidently engraved with a narrow chisel. Sa is one of the *jūtetsu* (ten brilliant pupils) of Masamune of Sagami province and his dated pieces include two *tantō* dated 1339. *Sa* is an abbreviation of Saemon Saburō and the first Sa is usually called "the Great Sa" to distinguish him from his numerous school. This, the best of his *tantō,* can be seen to have been one of Toyotomi Hideyoshi's treasures from its inclusion in the *Kōtoku oshigata,* a collection of blade drawings. It was subsequently worn by Tokugawa Hidetada.

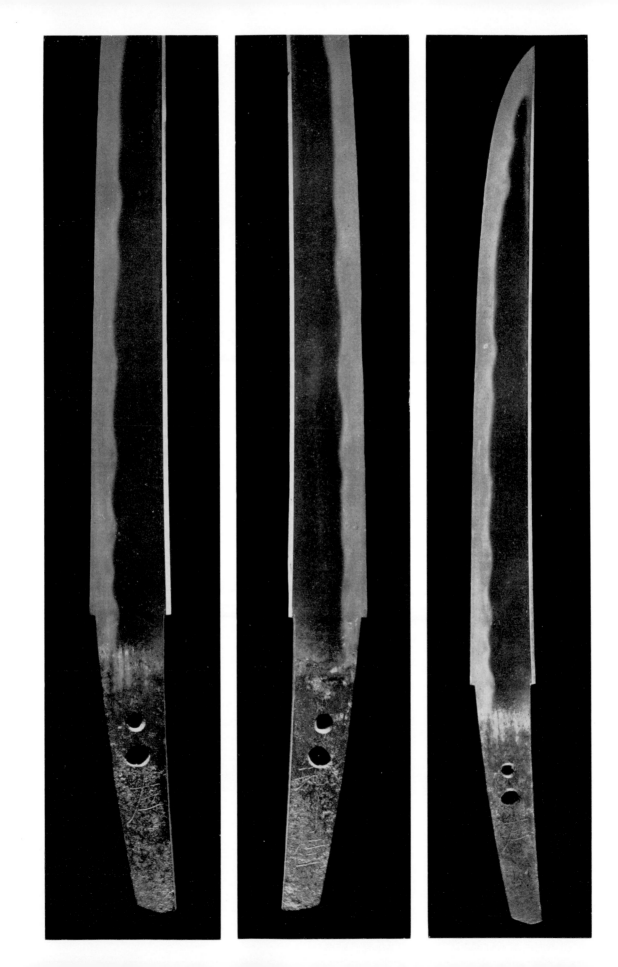

69. *Katana.* By Sukesada. Steel. *Nagasa* 70.6 cm. 1521. Collection of Okano Tarōmatsu.

BLADE: curve 1.9 cm. *Shinogi-zukuri, sakizori.*
GRAIN: extremely tight *koitame,* with fine *jinie.*
HAMON: lower part *chū-suguha,* upper part *gunome midare.* Bright *nioi* and many *konie* with *ashi* and *yō* over the whole and, in the upper part, *tobiyaki* (large areas of tempered metal on the main body).
BŌSHI: *midarekomi,* with deep turnback at the point.
TANG: *ubu.* Short, with *kurijiri* butt. Signed *Bizen no kuni no jū Osafune Yozō-saemon-no-jō Sukesada Kuriyama Yokurō no tame kore o saku* ("Osafune Yozō-saemon-no-jō Sukesada of Bizen province made this for Kuriyama Yokurō") on one side. Dated *Eishō jūhachinen kichinichi* ("On a lucky day in Eishō 18 [1521]") on the reverse.

KATANA, BY SUKESADA

This is a classic example of the *uchigatana* which came into use as companion swords to *tachi* during the Muromachi period (pl. 69). It is typical both in length and in the short and stubby tang which indicates that it must have been intended for use with one hand only. The *sakizori* curve is evidence that it was shaped so that drawing and striking could be accomplished in a single movement, *nukiuchi,* as mentioned earlier. The extra *mekugiana* at the butt, called *shinobiana,* is another practical feature: two pegs were used, and if one of them broke the sword would not fly out of the sheath. Such care in matters of detail is typical in swords which were made to order, as the inscription on the present blade indicates.

There were twenty or more smiths with the name Sukesada in the Muromachi period and of these the best were Yozō-saemon-no-jō, the maker of the blade illustrated here, Gembei-jō, and Hikobei-jō. This *katana* has always been considered the best of Yozō-saemon's works. Its wide *yakiba,* divided into *suguha* and lively *midareba,* is a feature which is not found on earlier swords.

70. "Yamaubagiri." *Katana.* By Kunihiro. Steel. *Nagasa* 69.9 cm. 1590. Collection of Ise Torahiko.

BLADE: curve 2.8 cm., *motohaba* 3.3 cm., *sakihaba* 2.9 cm., *kissaki* length 7.7 cm. *Shinogi-zukuri, sakizori, iorimune.*

GRAIN: mixture of *itame* and *mokume* with many *jinie, chikei, tobiyaki,* and *muneyaki.*

HAMON: abrupt *midare* with *gunome,* made up of rich *ashi, yō,* and *sunagashi* articulated with patches of *nie.*

BŌSHI: strong undulation. Includes scattered *nie* and throws *tobiyaki* into the rest of the *kissaki.*

TANG: *ubu.* Signed *Kyūshū Hyūga no jū Kunihiro saku* ("Made by Kunihiro of Hyūga in Kyushu"). Date *Tenshō jūhachinen kanoe-tora nigatsu kichinichi Taira no Akinaga* ("For Taira no Akinaga on a lucky day in the second month of Tenshō 18 [1590]").

KATANA, BY KUNIHIRO

This broad and powerful blade is rather thin, with grooves on both sides (pl. 70). The mixture of *itame* and *mokume* grain is very prominent and clear and flows smoothly over the whole surface. The *hamon* is particularly fine. Kunihiro, called Tanaka Shinano-no-kami, was a native of Obi in Hyūga province, Kyushu, and was originally a retainer of the Itō family, but after their demise he wandered from province to province practicing his craft. He is sometimes called the father of the *shintō* sword. Later in life he settled at Ichijō Horikawa in Kyoto and, as the founder of the Horikawa school, trained a great many distinguished pupils. This *katana* was made for Nagao Taira no Akinaga, lord of Ashikaga in Kazusa province, during Kunihiro's stay there in 1590, and is copied from a blade by Bizen Osafune Chōgi. The name Yamaubagiri originally belonged to the Chōgi sword but it passed to the Kunimitsu when the latter was made. As is to be expected the strength and splendor of the blade derive from its fourteenth century original. The *hamon* is particularly fine. The making of this blade made Kunihiro aware of the Sagami style (Chōgi being a pupil of Masamune), which became the main inspiration of the Horikawa school. Kunihiro never made a finer blade.

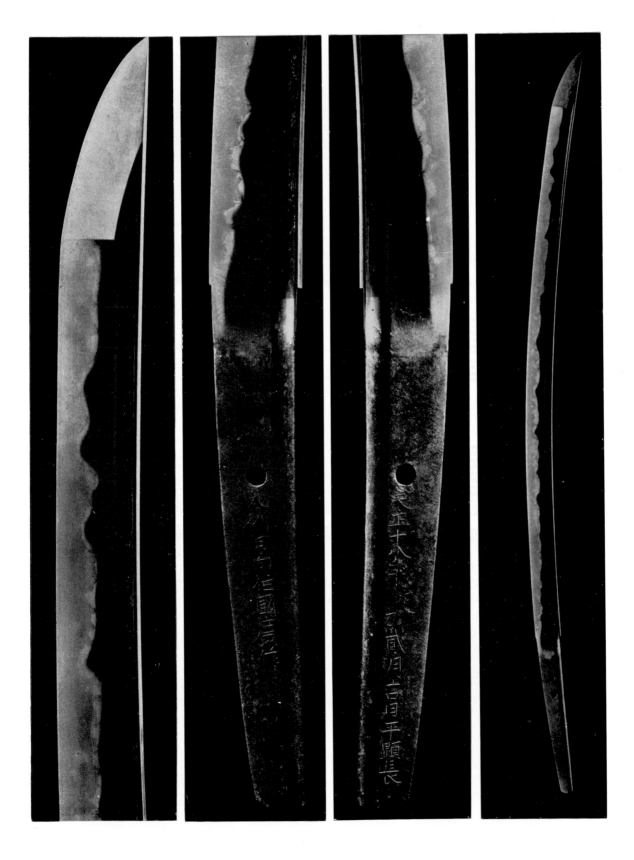

72. *Katana.* By Kiyomaro. Steel. *Nagasa* 80.2 cm. 1846. Collection of Ebara Shōichirō.

BLADE: curve 3.0 cm., *motohaba* 3.0 cm., *sakihaba* 2.4 cm. *Shinogi-zukuri, iorimune,* slightly extended *chū-kissaki.*

GRAIN: rich *chikei* and *jinie.*

HAMON: combines *notare* and *gunome* with dense *nioi,* extravagant *nie,* and frequent *kinsuji* and *sunagashi.*

BŌSHI: continues main *hamon* and ends in *komaru* turn-back.

TANG: *ubu.* Signed *Kubota Sugane no tame Yamaura Tamaki Minamoto no Kiyomaro sei* ("Made by Yamaura Tamaki Minamoto no Kiyomaro for Kubota Sugane"). Dated *Kōka hinoe-uma hachigatsu* ("Eighth month of Kōka, *hinoe-uma* year [1846]").

KATANA, BY KIYOMARO

This strongly curved blade (pl. 72) shows the influence of the style of the Nambokuchō period, especially as it appears in the swords of the Sagami tradition made by Shizu Saburō Kaneuji. Kiyomaro, who produced this blade, was born as Yamaura Tamaki in 1813, the son of a country samurai named Nobukaze who lived in Akaiwa village, part of Komoro in Shinano province. At first he was apprenticed to Kawamura Toshitaka, a swordsmith of Ueda near Komoro, and called himself Masayuki. In 1834, at the age of twenty-two, he decided to go to Edo, not to work as a swordsmith but to take advantage of the current interest in military philosophy and improve his understanding of *bushidō,* the samurai code, by studying under the famous and talented *hatamoto* (direct vassal of the shogun) and military theorist Kubota Sugane. Sugane recognized his pupil's talents as a swordsmith and, wishing to help him, in 1839 organized for his benefit a *bukikō,* a type of lottery in which one hundred men each paid three *ryō* and swords were shared among them. The venture failed and Kiyomaro, who had lost all his money, fled for a time to Nagato province. Later, however, he returned to Edo and with the help of Sugane he established a smithy at Igachō, Yotsuya. In 1846 he changed his name to Kiyomaro, and this blade, made as a gift for Sugane in the same year, is in every respect worthy of being regarded as his supreme masterpiece. On the strength of such work he came to be called "the Masamune of Yotsuya," but his brief period of production ended when he committed suicide in 1854, bringing his curious career to a close at the age of forty-two.

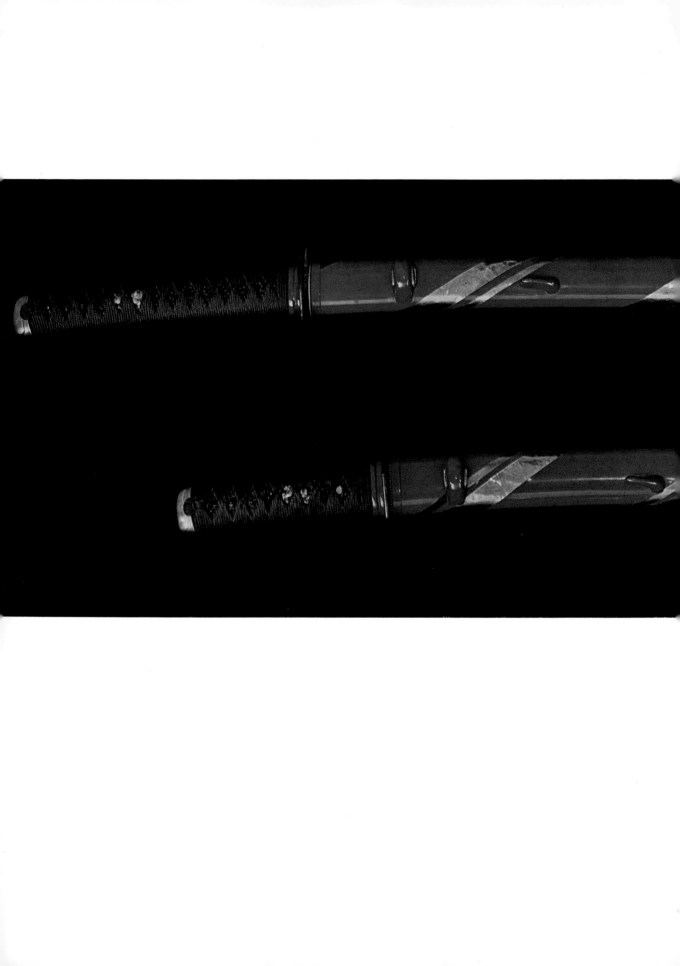

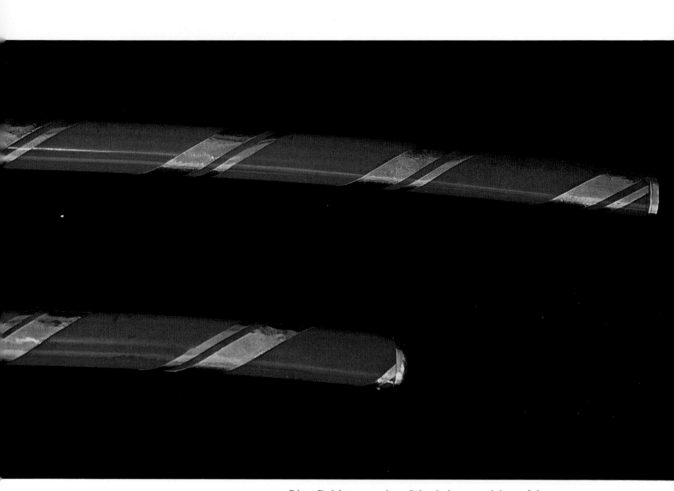

74. *Daishō* mounting. Wood decorated in red lacquer wound with gold foil; hilts wrapped in black-lacquered rayskin bound with silk bands; gold and *shakudō* fittings. L. 94.5 cm., 62.1 cm. Momoyama period. Tokyo National Museum.

This mounting was presented to Mizoguchi Hidekatsu (1538–1600) by Toyotomi Hideyoshi (1536–98) and is another example of the *daishō* style as it first appeared during the Momoyama period. The simple decoration with gold foil whose order is subtly reversed in the short sword exemplifies the geometrical boldness found in many of the decorative arts of the period.

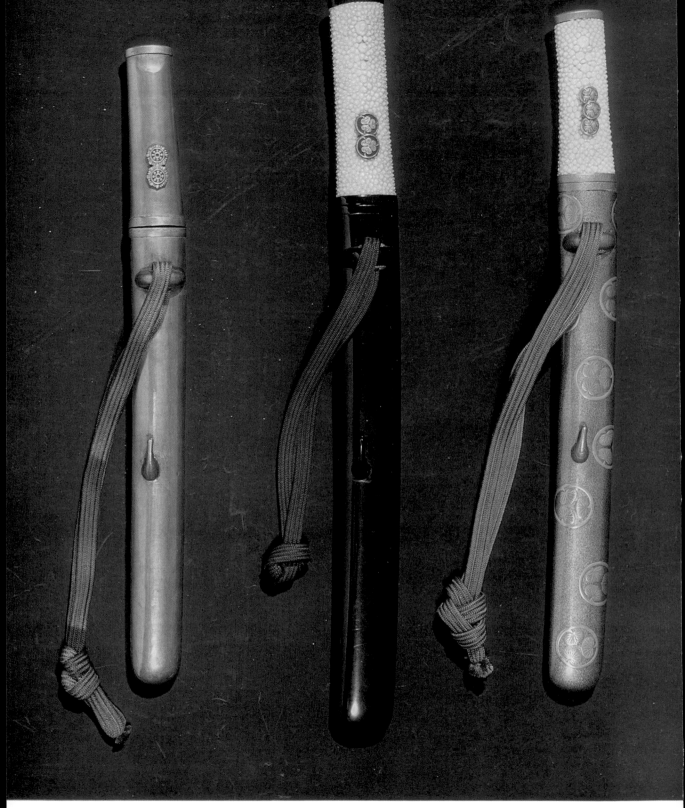

75. Mountings from the Momoyama or early Edo period. RIGHT: Guardless dagger mounting with hollyhock badge decoration. Wood decorated in *kinnashiji* (gold flakes suspended in lacquer); hilt wrapped in rayskin; gold fittings. L. 42.5 cm. Private collection. MIDDLE: Guardless dagger mounting. Wood, decorated with plain black lacquer; hilt wrapped in rayskin; gold and *shakudō* fittings. L. 47.0 cm. Tōshōgū, Tochigi Prefecture. LEFT: Guardless dagger mounting. Wood covered in gold foil (*kinnoshitsuki*); gold fittings. L. 39.7 cm. Okamiyama Shrine, Tottori Prefecture.

Examples of the guardless dagger types found after the Muromachi period, two with the characteristic unwrapped rayskin hilts. The range of designs found is very wide, depending mostly on the taste of the wearer, and later in the Edo period some very eccentric forms were developed.

3
___

THE MOUNTS OF A JAPANESE SWORD

The original purpose of sword mounts was the obvious one of protecting the sword from damage, but it was not long before they came, in addition, to symbolize a man's social status and add dignity to his appearance. The long and splendidly mounted *tachi* or *katana* that a warrior wore at his waist was a clear and unmistakable mark of his power, wealth, and courage. This chapter traces some of the different styles of sword mounting that came into being in response to historical changes and developments in fighting technique.

THE EARLY PERIOD

We can get some idea of the appearance of the earliest Japanese swords by looking at the swords worn by primitive peoples in other parts of the world today. Naturally these vary somewhat from country to country but, generally speaking, the earliest scabbards are made from wood, or from animal or fish skins bound together with plant tendrils or the like. It may be conjectured, however, that there were differences, even in these crude efforts, depending on the social status of the wearer. Given that human abilities do not really show great fundamental variety it seems certain that the primitive swords we see today, although of recent manufacture, developed from the same kind of conditions as their Japanese counterparts. In the *Nihon shoki* it is related that a certain Iiirine was tricked by his elder brother Izumo Furune into exchanging his own sword for the wooden one worn by the latter and subsequently killed as a result. At this point in the narrative there is the poem,

> Alas for Iiirine that the *tachi* which the warrior of cloudy Izumo wore, though splendidly wound round with creepers, had in it no true blade.

The fact that the writer specially mentions a mount "splendidly wound round with creepers" indicates that he regarded it as a sign of high rank.

128

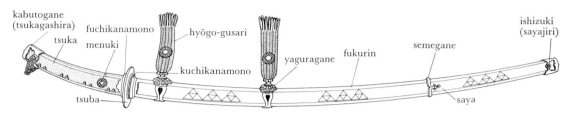

76. *Hyōgo-gusari tachi* mounting.

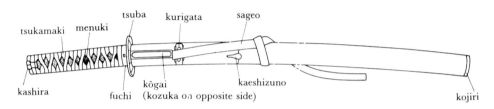

77. *Uchigatana* mounting.

FROM THE KOFUN PERIOD TO THE TWO-SWORD STYLE

Among the objects excavated from the tumuli of the Kofun period (A.D. 250 552) there are *tachi* of *kabutsuchi* (hammer-headed), *kantō* (ring-headed), and *keitō* (jewel-headed) type. *Kantō no tachi* (*tachi* with ring-pommels; pls. 18, 93) were introduced from the mainland and seem to have been in use for a comparatively long period. In the *Man'yōshū* and other poetry collections, expressions like *Koma tsurugi* ("sword from Korea") are frequently encountered but they are simply a conventional reading of the word *wa* meaning "wheel" or "ring" and referring to the ring decorated with pierced designs which was fitted to the end of the hilt. Of the various designs found in these ring-pommels the dragon is the commonest. Examples in which the carved design has volume and appears almost in the round (called *nikubori*) are earlier and of superior craftsmanship while those in which the design is cut out in profile from a thin sheet of metal (*itagane*) are inferior. The *kabutsuchi* and *keitō* types (pl. 93) are both thought to be of native Japanese origin. The *kabutsuchi* is a large fitting recalling in shape a fist clasping the end of the hilt while the *keitō* narrows off towards its base and is similar in shape to the top of a Japanese chess, or *shōgi*, piece.

When we look at them today these fittings seem very impractical, but if we bear in mind that at the time they were used swords were probably wielded with one hand only we can see that without the additional weight they gave at the end of the hilt the blade could not have been adequately balanced. It is likely that they were also important for their decorative effect and their contribution to the dignified appearance of the wearer.

In these early mounts the scabbard and hilt are made of wood covered with a thin sheet of metal which is held in place by ring-shaped fittings known as *semegane*, dec-

129

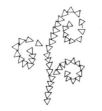

78. Pattern in *keribori*.

orated in repoussé work or in a technique known as *keribori* (see pl. 78), in which the individual strokes of the chisel do not form a continuous line and are clearly visible. The metal is also gilded and the whole assemblage is a magnificent sight. The guards, or *tsuba*, are egg-shaped and pierced to resemble a spoked wheel (pl. 94); some are made from plain iron but the majority are finely gilded or silvered. There exists a portrait (pl. 19) which, according to tradition, represents either Asa Taishi, son of a Korean king, or Shōtoku Taishi (574–622), the great statesman and reformer. It is one of the objects which was dedicated to the Hōryū-ji temple and is now in the care of the Imperial Household Agency. The painting shows Shōtoku Taishi, if that is who it is, in the center with a prince in attendance on either side of him. Although it does not date from his lifetime it is believed by specialists to have been executed not much later. We can see from this picture that Shōtoku and the two princes are all wearing *tachi*. But these *tachi*, as painted, look very peculiar. No *tachi* mounts of this shape or anything like it have survived to the present day, although it may be that they are based on some old Korean pattern. In any case the straps attaching the *tachi* to the belts of the two princes in particular exhibit a number of quite impractical-looking features and altogether the appearance of the metal fittings and the *tsuba* present serious problems. It is also difficult to see how the swords would have been drawn. The portrait does, however, at least enable us to guess at the way the *tachi* of that time were worn, and from this point of view it is a most valuable document.

79. Detail of reproduction of a portrait of Fujiwara no Kamatari. Color on paper. Original
not extant, probably produced mid-nineteenth
century. Tokyo National Museum.

Much vital evidence for the history of Japanese sword mounts is provided by the
many splendid examples, such as the Chinese-style *tachi* with decoration in gold,
silver, and mother-of-pearl, which have been preserved in the Shōsō-in. During the
Nara period there were many advances in the art of lacquering and a number of
extremely sophisticated new techniques were devised, for example *heidatsu*, which is
the inlay of thin pieces of cut sheet metal into wet lacquer, and *saie*, which combines
colored lacquers and gold and silver dust. At the same time great ingenuity was
displayed in the working of the metal fittings and in the inlay technique known as
hirazōgan, in which the surface of the metal is cut out in the desired design and filled
with another metal, after which the whole surface is made flat again. Gold, silver,
and gilding were also used. In contrast with the preceding period, *kabutsuchi* and *keitō*
pommels are no longer found and *tsuba* become smaller and appear for the first time
in the *shitogi* ("rice-cake") shape. But in contrast with later times the *mekugi* peg is
hardly used, the blade being held in place by a cord known as *tenuki no o* which was
passed through the tang.

In the Heian period a system developed under which a sharp distinction was made
between swords designed for actual use in battle and those whose purpose was purely
ceremonial. The tradition of the Chinese-style *tachi* was carried on by the ceremonial
sword of the type known as *kazaritachi* ("decorative sword"), which has a straight
blade formed from a crudely hammered out piece of iron with no sharpened edge,
clearly unsuitable for actual use. Because their blades are very narrow compared to
those of practical *tachi*, these swords are also known as *hosodachi* ("narrow *tachi*").
Beautiful fittings, on which skillful craftsmanship was lavished, were used to enhance
the external appearance of these weapons. Two fittings known as *yamagatakanamono*
("mountain-shaped" metal fitting) were provided to hold the straps (*obitori*) which
secured the sword to the wearer's belt, and the length of the scabbard between
them was covered by another fitting known as the *tsutsukanamono* ("tube" fitting).
As well as these there were the ring-shaped *semegane* mentioned above. These metal
fittings were decorated with crystals and other precious jewels and stones, the hilt
was in rayskin, which was not wrapped as in later times, and the scabbard was decorated in mother-of-pearl and *makie* lacquer with designs such as the long-tailed
birds in plates 20 and 21.

There were, of course, differences in the style of mounting depending on social
position, starting from the emperor, members of the Fujiwara line of imperial regents,
and other people of high standing and descending to those of inferior rank. The
swords worn by such people had rougher metal fittings and instead of the *tsutsukanamono* arrangement there were two separate *ashikanagu* ("foot metal" fittings). The
kazaritachi style was used by nobles for ceremonial court purposes until the Muromachi period. A copy in the Tokyo National Museum of a portrait of the statesman
Fujiwara no Kamatari (614–69; pl. 79) shows us how these swords were worn.

131

At some time, probably about the middle of the Heian period, a new style of mounting with a pierced hilt, the *kenukigata no tachi*, became fashionable (pls. 80–82). The best of the very few examples surviving today is probably that in the Kasuga Shrine at Nara, which is decorated in mother-of-pearl and *makie* lacquer with a lively design of sparrows among bamboos. Unfortunately its blade is rusted firmly in and cannot be withdrawn. In the Chōkokan museum attached to the Ise Shrine in Mie Prefecture there is another *kenukigata no tachi* whose scabbard is wrapped in red brocade held in place with metal fittings and whose hilt has the same "hair tweezer" shape (pl. 28). The blade has been extensively polished down at some time but it is fairly close in style to the swords in the Shōsō-in and certainly earlier than the time of the swordsmiths Munechika and Yasutsuna. It is *shinogi-zukuri* but the ridge lies rather near the center of the sides. The metal has a large, clear *itame* grain and the *hamon* is *hososuguha* with only slight *notare*. It exhibits the brushed effect known as *hotsure* and includes *konie*. The strongly curved appearance of this blade is due not to the curve in its cutting part, which is only slight, but to the sudden bend in the tang. The Ise *tachi* is said to have been used by the Fujiwara chieftain Tawara Tōta Hidesato (tenth century). In the Temmangū at Dazaifu there is another *kenukigata no tachi* said to have been used by the celebrated statesman and man of letters Sugawara Michizane (845–903), but this has been damaged by fire and has no mounts. The same is unfortunately true of the sword said to have been used by Tsunemori of the powerful Taira clan (1125–85), which is now in the temple on the island of Chikubushima in Lake Biwa.

The hilt of the *kenukigata no tachi*, pierced in the center with a large hair-tweezer shape, is made in one piece with the rest of the sword. It is fitted with an ornamental border and has no separate wooden covering. From the portraits attributed to Fujiwara no Takanobu (1141–1205) of Minamoto no Yoritomo (1147–99; pls. 83, 84), Taira no Shigemori (1137–79), and Fujiwara no Mitsuyoshi it is clear that swords in this style of mounting were used, like the *kazaritachi*, for ceremonial purposes, but the Ise Chōkokan example, which has marks of blows from swords on its back, shows that they were also used in warfare.

80. *Kenukigata no tachi* mounting. Scabbard decorated in gold lacquer, shell, and green enamel, with gilt fittings; hilt covered in gilt metal. L. 96.3 cm. Mid-Heian period. Kasuga Shrine, Nara.

81–82. Details of *kenukigata no tachi* shown in plate 80. Kasuga Shrine, Nara.

Of the few sword mountings surviving from the Heian period the *tachi* wrapped in a continuous band of silvered copper and decorated with hexagonal patterns in the possession of the Nibutsuhime Shrine, Wakayama, is an important example (pls. 22, 23). In this durable mounting, which originally contained a narrow blade, the black-lacquered base is wound round and round with a long narrow strip of silvered copper and all the other mounts are worked with a hexagonal pattern, including the guard, which has it on its edge. The beautiful hilt, which is strongly curved and widens towards its end, is covered in black-lacquered rayskin, and the fitting covering the end (*kabutogane*) and the decorative studs (*kazaribyō*) are all worked in the same hexagonal pattern. There is no blade, but judging from the shape of the mounting, there was a sharp bend in the area below the hilt while the cutting part of the sword was only very slightly curved. It can be inferred, therefore, that these swords herald the appearance on the scene of the later *koshizori* shape.

In the Sanage Shrine in Aichi Prefecture is a *tachi* by Namihira Yukiyasu which is a particularly fine specimen of the work of the Namihira line of Heian-period smiths (pls. 85, 86). The surface of the blade is almost soft and porous in appearance and has a whitish look about it; the *hamon* is a beautiful *hososuguha* and the tang, which is in the *kijimomo* shape, has a rather thickly chiseled two-character signature *Yukiyasu*. The mounts consist of a hilt wrapped with a gilt bronze band and a sheath whose *hyōgo-gusari* fittings (see below) are unfortunately missing. The sword as a whole may be compared with the previous example. It can be inferred from the existence of these two swords that mounts wrapped with a band of silver were fashionable for a time.

From the close of the Heian period into the Kamakura period, the fashionable style of *tachi* was the *nagafukurin hyōgo-gusari*, which takes the *hyōgo-gusari* ("*hyōgo* chains") part of its name from the special woven-chain technique used in making the *obitori* straps or slings (pls. 24, 25). The *hyōgo* part of the name comes from the arsenal (*bukikō* or *hyōgo*) at court in which weapons were stored. The gorgeous and majestic appearance of the *nagafukurin no tachi* (*tachi* with long ornamental border), which was decorated around the edge of both scabbard and hilt with a long ornamental border, is reflected in the late Heian chronicles such as the accounts of the Hōgen and Heiji insurrections by the use of the term *ikamono-zukuri tachi* ("*tachi* of ferocious make").

There can be no doubt that this style of mounting, which was used by high-ranking generals when they were wearing armor, was designed for use in battle, but probably because of their gorgeous appearance swords decorated in the *hyōgo-gusari* style came in the Kamakura period to be made exclusively for dedication at temples and shrines; consequently the blades used in them were unserviceable lengths of dull, hammered-out iron (pls. 50–51). The construction of the woven chains became simpler, losing its former elegance, and in the Nambokuchō period mounts of this type were used in a general way for all outsize *tachi*. But throughout this time the chains retain their characteristic tapering outline. Examples of this style survive in the Futarasan Shrine

83. Portrait of Minamoto no Yoritomo. Attributed to
Fujiwara no Takanobu. Color on silk. H. 139.4 cm. Ca.
1200. Jingo-ji, Kyoto.

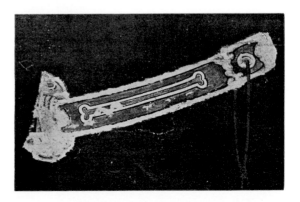

84. Detail of plate 83, showing the hilt of the *kenukigata
no tachi*.

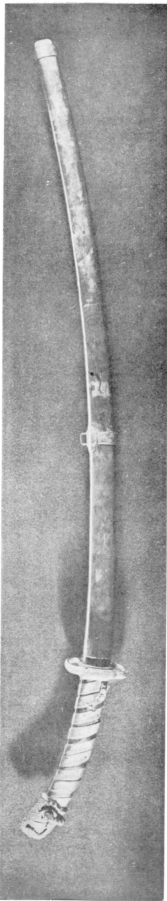

85. *Hyōgo-gusari tachi* mounting. Hilt wood covered in a gilt bronze band with carved mounts. L. 102.0 cm. Late Heian period. Sanage Shrine, Aichi Prefecture.

86. *Tachi.* Signed *Yukiyasu.* The blade for the mounting shown in plate 85. Steel. *Nagasa* 70.9 cm. Late Heian period. Sanage Shrine, Aichi Prefecture.

at Nikkō in Tochigi Prefecture and in the Kasuga Shrine at Nara, and in other places.

In contrast to the rather ostentatious styles mentioned so far was a simple type known as *kurourushi* ("black lacquer"; pls. 87, 88). A plain black-lacquered scabbard had been a category of mounting since the Nara period and in the Heian and Kamakura periods it came, it seems, to be used by brave warriors. Its special features include the jet-black *yakiurushi* technique of lacquering, in which the lacquer is burnt onto the ground, used on the various fittings as well as on the scabbard; the *tsuba*, called *kawa-tsuba* ("leather *tsuba*"), which is a flat guard made up of several layers of leather hardened with black lacquer; and the use of leather for the *obitori* slings, all of which give it a less ferocious appearance than the *hyōgo-gusari* mounts. Because of its cheapness and simplicity this type was probably very popular.

Although the black-lacquered style continued into the Nambokuchō period it became the practice then to wrap the scabbard in unstretched tanned leather which retained its natural wrinkled look. There are two subdivisions of this style: sometimes the fittings are concealed under the leather and sometimes they protrude. The former is called *onimaru-zukuri* after a *tachi* called Onimaru by Kunitsuna which is mounted in that style. Another mounting of this type, used by Ashikaga Takauji and subsequently dedicated at the Atago Shrine in Kyoto, is known as the *sasamaru* mounting because the *ashikanagu* and all the other attached fittings are decorated with bamboo (*sasa*) designs (pl. 52). These mountings are remarkable for the special bag which covers the guard and is attached at one end to the hilt. It was designed to protect the leather guard from being damaged by getting wet in snow or rain while the sword was in use in battle. It seems that brown leather as well as black-lacquered leather was used for the wrappings of the mounts during this period.

Black-lacquered *tachi* mounts continued to be fashionable during the Muromachi period and there are *koshigatana* with black-lacquered scabbards. In the Edo period mounted *daishō* pairs of *katana* and *wakizashi* decorated in *kuroironuri*, a technique of black lacquering which gives a shiny finish, were used as a ceremonial style by the

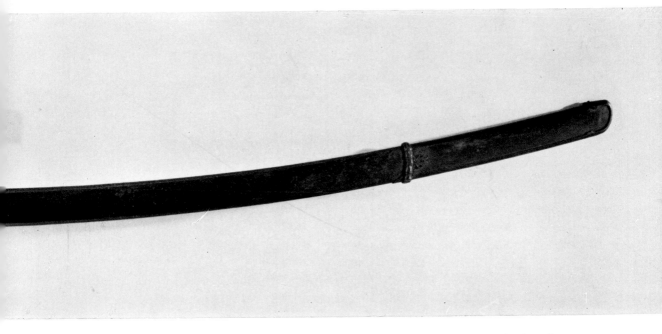

87. "Kitsunegasaki." *Tachi* mounting said to have been
used at the battle of Kitsunegasaki in 1200. Scabbard
black lacquer on leather-wrapped wood; hilt black-
lacquered leather band; copper fittings. *Nagasa* of blade
78.8 cm. Kamakura period. Tokyo National Museum.

88. Detail of *tachi* shown in plate 87.

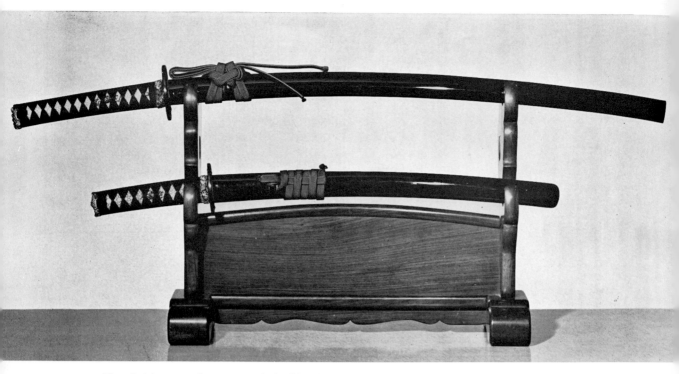

89. *Daishō* mounting on stand. Scabbard black lacquer; hilt rayskin wrapped in black thread with *shakudō* and gold fittings. L. 95.4 cm., 66.1 cm. Edo period. Tokyo National Museum.

samurai class (pls. 89, 90). Special features of the most formal type, as illustrated in plate 89, include the metal fittings of *shakudō* and gold made by members of the Gotō family (see the following chapter), the butt-piece cut straight in the long sword and rounded in the short sword, and the way in which the silk ribbon is threaded through the horn eyelet on the sheath. During the Momoyama and Edo periods it became fashionable for the hilts of *koshigatana* mounted in *aikuchi* style (i.e., without the guard) to be left unwrapped, with the rayskin and the small fittings called *menuki* showing, and the wrapped style of *aikuchi* which had been current since the Nambokuchō period (pl. 53) was largely abandoned.

As well as black lacquer a number of other techniques which gave a splendid effect were in vogue among the daimyo, among them *kinnoshitsuki*, in which a thin sheet of hammered gold is wrapped around the scabbard; *kinikakeji*, in which gold lacquer is applied to the whole surface of the scabbard; and *kinnashiji*, in which flakes of gold are set at differing angles in wet lacquer, covered with more lacquer, and polished (pl. 75). Plate 91 shows two of the more unusual styles of mounting prevalent in Higo province, Kyushu. The wickerwork mounting, consisting of a cane scabbard bound in wickerwork with austere metal fittings, was used by Katō Kiyomasa and is now in the Hommyō-ji, Kumamoto Prefecture. The mounting with impressed ribbing was owned by the warlord Hosokawa Sansai Tadaoki (1563–1645). Another type of mounting, such as was used by daimyo on non-formal occasions, is shown in plate 92. The metal fittings used in these newer styles of mount underwent a transformation from the almost static style of the old *tachi* fittings to the free designs of fittings used for *uchigatana* swords. This transformation is discussed in the next chapter.

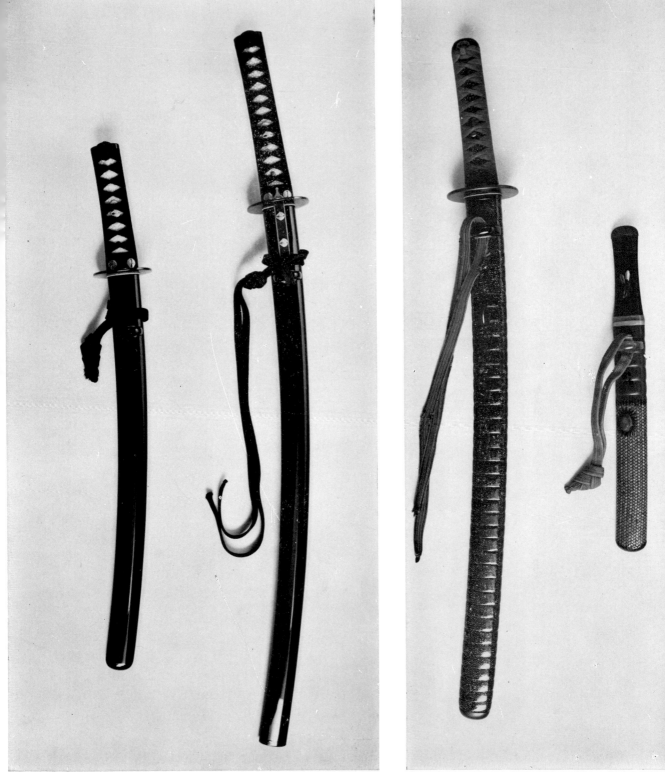

90. *Daishō* mounting. Scabbard black lacquer; hilt rayskin wrapped in black thread with *shakudō* and gold fittings. L. 89.0 cm., 63.0 cm. Edo period. Tokyo National Museum.

91. RIGHT: Reproduction of a *koshigatana* mounted in wickerwork in the Hommyō-ji, Kumamoto Prefecture. Hilt rust-colored lacquer. L. 37.2 cm. Original late sixteenth century. LEFT: Reproduction of an *uchigatana* mounting. Scabbard black-lacquered sharkskin with impressed ribbing; hilt black-lacquered sharkskin with brown leather thread; *shakudō* fittings. L. 75.0 cm. Collection of Ōtsuki Takaharu.

92. *Daishō* mounting. Scabbard lacquer; hilt rayskin wrapped in mottled leather. Edo period. Private collection.

93. ABOVE AND BELOW RIGHT: *Kantō no tachi* pommels. L. 14.6 cm., 8.0 cm. BELOW LEFT: *Keitō no tachi* pommel. L. 6.6 cm. Gilt bronze. Fourth century A.D. Tokyo National Museum.
These pommels are examples of the earliest metal sword-fittings to have survived in Japan.

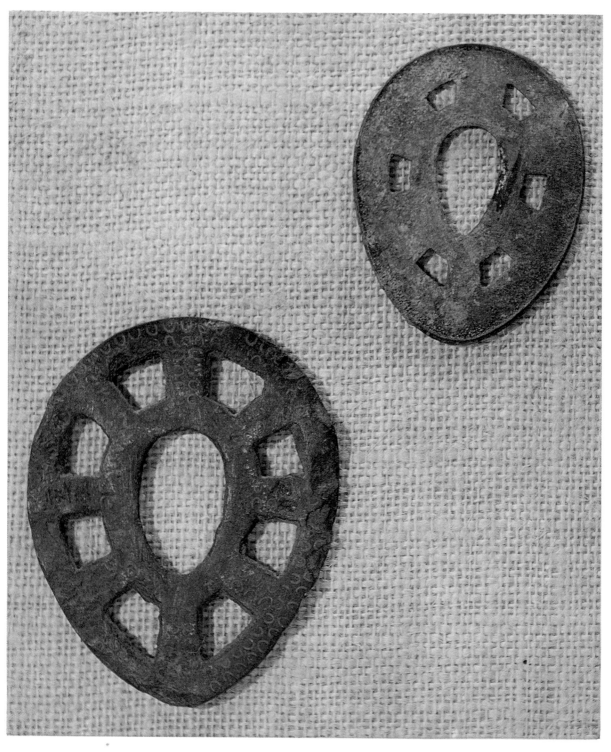

94. ABOVE: Copper-gilt guard (*tsuba*) for a *tachi*.
Shown actual size. BELOW: Iron guard for a
tachi with silver inlay. Shown actual size. Kofun
period. Tokyo National Museum.
Guards such as these were fitted to swords along
with the pommels reproduced in plate 93.

95. RIGHT: Sword guard with design of Kasuga-no. Signed *Jōshū Fushimi no jū Kaneie* ("Kaneie of Fushimi in Yamashiro province"). Iron with silver inlay, copper fittings, and *shibuichi* plugs; copper at top and bottom of central hole to tighten sword in guard. D. 8.0 cm. Eisei Bunko, Tokyo. LEFT: Sword guard with design of monkey reaching for the moon's reflection. Signed *Yamashiro no kuni Fushimi no jū Kaneie* ("Kaneie of Fushimi in Yamashiro province"). Iron with gold and silver inlay and *shakudō* plugs. D. 9.0 cm. Collection of Taguchi Minoru. Both guards late Muromachi period.

Kaneie is generally regarded as the father of pictorial style in sword guards. These two pieces represent the two sources on which he drew for his designs. The landscape with deer is based on similar designs in lacquer, themselves taking their subject matter from literature. It shows the area around the Kasuga Shrine in Nara, which is still famous for its deer. The monkey reaching for the moon's reflection is a Zen Buddhist theme derived from imported Chinese paintings and their Japanese copies. The pieces of copper in the central opening of the Kasuga guard are later additions to enable the guard to be mounted on a slightly smaller blade. The plugs are also later additions, fitted when the guards were included in mountings that did not have a *kozuka* or *kōgai* (see pl. 103).

96. Sword guard with design of broken fans and falling cherry blossoms. By Hayashi Matashichi. Iron with gold overlay; *shakudō* plug. D. 8.5 cm. Seventeenth century. Eisei Bunko, Tokyo.

Hayashi Matashichi (1605[1613?]–91[99?]) was the founder of the Hayashi school, one of four groups which made Higo province an important center of sword-fitting manufacture. Like many of his coprovincials he worked in the service of the Hosokawa family of daimyo. He is famous for his skill in the application of gold overlay, in which the soft metal is hammered onto shallow grooves cut in the iron as a key. Both broken fans and falling cherry blossoms symbolize the Buddhist concept of impermanence; the cherry blossoms also symbolize the warrior's selfless sacrifice of his life in the service of his lord.

97. Sword guard with grape vine and trellis design. Signed *Umetada Myōju*. Brass with gold, silver, and *shakudō*; silver plugs. D. 7.6 cm. Early seventeenth century. Collection of Mori Eiichi. Umetada Myōju (1558–1631) was famous both as a swordsmith and as a maker of fittings and was probably the first to use soft metals in a different style from that which had been made official by the Gotō school. His skillful use of a few different metals to achieve a rich polychromatic effect is typical of the Momoyama period and has much in common with the celebrated Kōdai-ji lacquers.

98. Sword guard with bow-and-arrow design.
By Hirata Hikozō (d. 1635). Copper with enamel
inlay. D. 7.5 cm. Early seventeenth century. Collection of Watanabe Kunio.

99. Sword guard with floral and cloud design.
By Hirata Dōjin. Iron with translucent cloisonné
enamels separated by gilt wire. D. 8.2 cm. Early
seventeenth century. Tokyo National Museum.

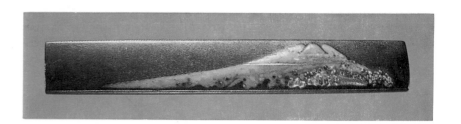

100. *Kozuka* with design of Mount Fuji. By Hirata Dōjin. *Shakudō* with translucent enamels separated by gilt wire. L. 9.7 cm. Early seventeenth century. Collection of Watanabe Kunio.

101. Pair of *menuki* with design of Mount Fuji. By Hirata Dōjin. Enamels on a metal base with gilt wire. Shown actual size. Early seventeenth century. Collection of Watanabe Kunio.

102. Sword guard with floral design. Signed *Hirata Hikoshirō* (=Dōjin). *Shakudō* with translucent enamels separated by gilt wire. D. 6.6 cm. Early seventeenth century. Tokyo National Museum.

Although numbers 99–101 are unsigned, they have been traditionally ascribed to Hirata Dōjin (1591–1646), the founder of the Hirata school whose pupils appear to have been active in the manufacture of enameled sword-fittings and other small items throughout the Edo period. The introduction of enamels is an expression, like the soft metals used by Umetada Myōju (pl. 97), of the penchant for bright colors which characterizes Momoyama taste.

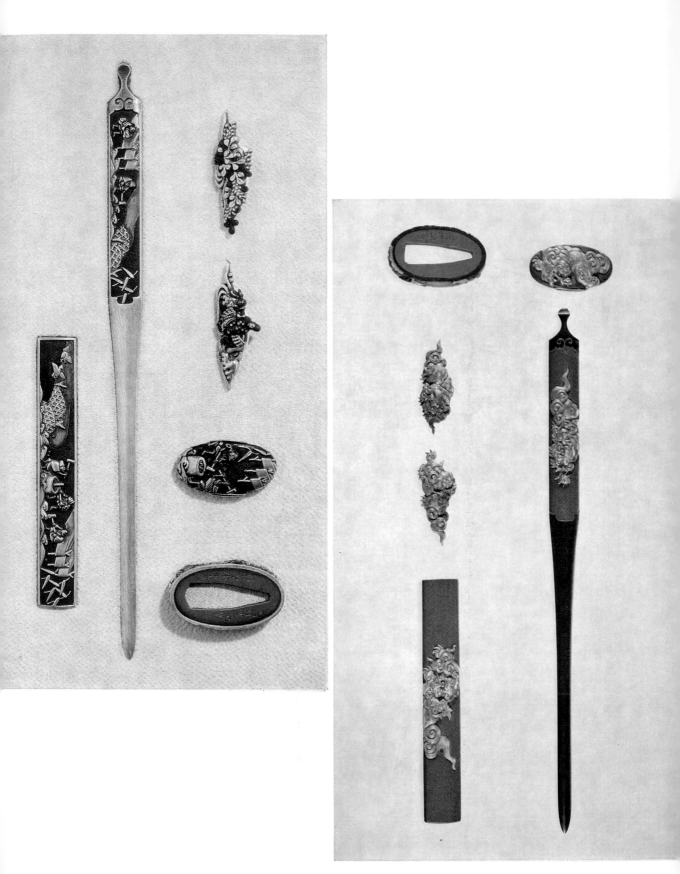

103.   *Mitokoromono* (set of *kozuka*, *kōgai*, and pair of *menuki*) with design of the Six Pearl Rivers. By Gotō Renjō. *Shakudō* with gold and silver; *fuchi* (collar) with copper plate. L. of *kōgai* 23.0 cm. Early Edo period. Collection of Fujii Manabu.

This is the masterpiece of Gotō Renjō (1627–1708), tenth master of the Gotō school. As usual the subject matter is traditional and has a literary origin. The set is executed in the usual Gotō techniques of gold and silver on a background of the blue-black alloy of copper and gold called *shakudō* which is worked with a regular pattern of minute granulations. The rectangular piece is the *kozuka*, the handle of a small dagger carried in the scabbard of the main sword. Next to it is the *kōgai*, a skewer carried on the opposite side of the scabbard. The two pieces at bottom right are the *fuchi* and *kashira*, the collar and the pommel, usually of uniform design, which fit over the two ends of the hilt. Above them are the *menuki*, which are held to the sides of the hilt by the silk wrapping.

104.   *Mitokoromono* with design of *shishi* (lion-dog) and peonies. By Yokoya Sōmin. *Shakudō* with gold and silver. L. of *kōgai* 21.0 cm. Early eighteenth century. Collection of Furukawa Junnosuke.

Yokoya Sōmin (1670–1733) is celebrated as the leader of the movement which broke away from the artistic tyranny of the Gotō school, a change which reflects a shift in patronage from samurai to rich townsmen. As with most of Sōmin's work, the subject matter is selected for its susceptibility to lively interpretation, and the well-worn theme is treated with more expressiveness than we would expect in a Gotō piece.

151

4

METAL SWORD-FITTINGS

The *tsuba* (guards) and other sword fittings which are most admired today were made for *uchigatana* and date from the late Muromachi onwards, the majority of them being of Momoyama- or Edo-period date. The reason for this is simple: very few *tachi* mounts made before that date survive today and those that do survive, although they vary in quality, differ very little from each other in form and style by comparison with the later fittings. The first *tsuba* are said to have been made by swordsmiths to go with their own swords. Some of the examples which we see today bear out the truth of this tradition, although we cannot be sure that they were exclusively the work of swordsmiths. Nevertheless, it is clear that such guards were considered by their makers to be adequate if they fulfilled their practical function, and no additional, aesthetic criteria were applied to their design or manufacture since, in any case, the techniques required for more elaborate decoration were not available before the emergence of specialist sword-fitting makers.

ARMORERS' TSUBA

The specialist manufacturers were preceded by armorers and others who made *tsuba* as a sideline. The armorers were able to apply the techniques involved in making the small-plates for armor directly to the manufacture of guards, adding sparse decoration in the form of pierced motifs (pls. 105, 106). They subsequently developed a range of designs with symbolic meanings, many of which were later taken over by the specialist schools. For example, a guard with a pierced design of a shell, *kai*, refers to the word *kai* meaning "success" and is thus a humble prayer for the success of an enterprise or a human life, while a design of the sun, moon, and stars expresses the hope that they will shine on mankind's efforts. The religious beliefs of the makers of these *tsuba* are also expressed by pierced inscriptions of Buddhist prayers, for example *Namu Amida butsu* ("Hail to Amitabha Buddha") and *Namu Hachiman dai bosatsu* ("Hail to the great bodhisattva Hachiman"). These early armorers' guards are mostly round and well forged. They are never signed.

105. Armorer's sword guard (*tsuba*) with pierced pagoda and sickle design. Iron. D. 10.5 cm. Muromachi period. Collection of Matsumoto Kintarō.

EARLY TSUBA-MAKERS

During the late Muromachi period the guards made as a sideline by armorers, sword-smiths, and mirror makers no longer provided an adequate supply and as a result specialist *tsuba*-makers emerged. Owari province was a leading center of activity in this field, and there exists a large group of unsigned guards with extensive piercing called *Owari sukashi* ("Owari piercing"). Nobuie (pls. 107–9) is the most important of the early *tsuba*-makers whose names are known. The signature probably represents a group of individuals working in several provinces rather than a single person, and it is no longer thought that the Nobuie represented by the signatures on *tsuba* is the same as Nobuie the armorer, seventeenth master of the Myōchin school who worked for the Takeda family of Kai province. Of the three pieces reproduced here, the guard in plate 109 with the *mitsudomoe* ("three comma") design is earlier than the other two. Like the armorers, Nobuie often inscribed poems expressing the samurai ideal on his *tsuba*, for example, "to be under crossed swords is hell, to make a sudden attack is heaven," or fatalistic mottoes such as *Un wa ten ni ari* ("Fate lies with heaven") in *kebori*, an engraving technique which produces a thin line in which no metal is removed from the surface (pl. 107).

Another important early *tsuba*-maker, living in Owari province, was Hōan (pl. 110). His guards are thick, with heavy piercing, and the iron is well forged, the grain of the metal being clearly visible, a typical feature of Owari work. A *tsuba* with wheel piercing, resembling the one reproduced here, can be seen in a Nambokuchō-period portrait of a warrior, said to be Ashikaga Takauji, and the design continued to be fashionable. In the Muromachi period there are pieces by Nobuie and Yamakichibei (another Owari worker) in the same style, and it was also copied by Umetada Myōju in the Momoyama period (pl. 114).

153

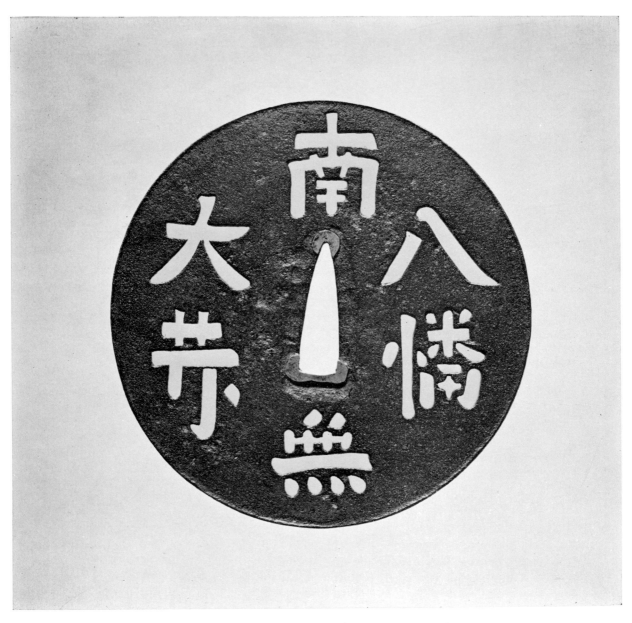

106. Armorer's sword guard with pierced inscription
Namu Hachiman dai bosatsu ("Hail to the great bodhisattva
Hachiman"). Iron. Muromachi period. Private collec-
tion.

107. Sword guard with bow-and-arrows design. Signed
Nobuie and incised on the reverse, with the inscription
Namu Hachiman dai bosatsu ("Hail to the great bodhisattva
Hachiman.") Iron. D. 8.5 cm. Late Muromachi period.
Collection of Watanabe Kunio.

108. Sword guard with pierced design of Christian
emblems. Signed *Nobuie*. Iron. D. 9.2 cm. Late Muromachi period. Tokyo National Museum.

155

109. Sword guard with pierced *mitsudomoe* design. Signed *Nobuie*. Iron. D. 8.6 cm. Late Muromachi period. Tokyo National Museum.

110. Sword guard with pierced wheel design. Signed *Hōan*. Iron. D. 8.6 cm. Late Muromachi period. Tokyo National Museum.

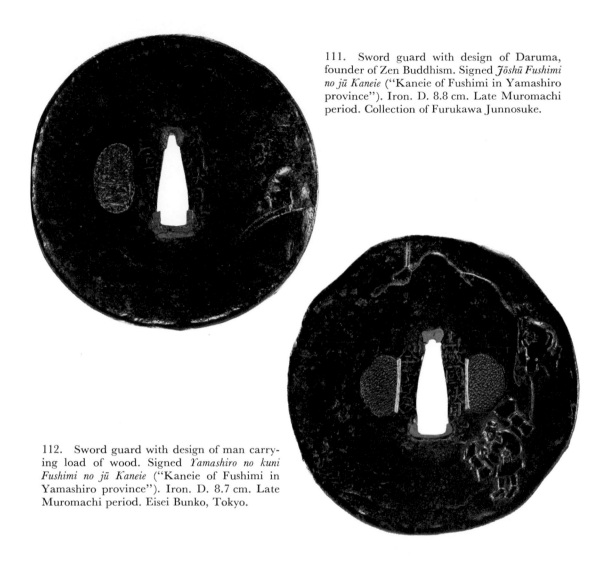

111. Sword guard with design of Daruma, founder of Zen Buddhism. Signed *Jōshū Fushimi no jū Kaneie* ("Kaneie of Fushimi in Yamashiro province"). Iron. D. 8.8 cm. Late Muromachi period. Collection of Furukawa Junnosuke.

112. Sword guard with design of man carrying load of wood. Signed *Yamashiro no kuni Fushimi no jū Kaneie* ("Kaneie of Fushimi in Yamashiro province"). Iron. D. 8.7 cm. Late Muromachi period. Eisei Bunko, Tokyo.

KANEIE

Guards may be divided into two groups: those with pictorial decoration and those formed into an overall design. Kaneie, who lived at Fushimi in Yamashiro province, is the founder and supreme master of the first group and, with the possible exception of Tsuchiya Yasuchika (see below), he has no equal. His designs recall the style of the monk-painters of the Muromachi period such as Sesshū and Shūbun and are executed in such techniques as *sukidashibori*, in which the metal of the ground is cut away, leaving the design in high relief; *iroe*, in which metals other than iron, such as gold, silver, *shakudō*, and copper, are used to color the design; and *zōgan*, inlay of a metal different from the principal metal of the guard. Kaneie produced very fine work and was especially skillful in obtaining striking effects by the use of the lightest touches of gold (pls. 95, 111, 112).

157

113. Irregular edge used
by Umetada Myōju.

114. Sword guard with pierced wheel design. Signed
Umetada Myōju. Iron with gold inlay. D. 7.9 cm. Momoyama period. Collection of Furukawa Junnosuke.

UMETADA MYŌJU

Umetada Myōju lived at Nishijin, Yamashiro province. His family was said to be
descended from the early smith Munechika. At first he was called Muneyoshi and
made swords for the shogunal family, but later he retired, taking the name of Myōju,
and made a thorough study of the techniques of metal carving, which eventually
became his chief specialty. Only his *tsuba* (apart from his swords) survive today, but
his successors made other fittings. Myōju imitated in his *tsuba* the decorative style of
the screen paintings of the Momoyama period, sometimes producing as many as
ten different colors on a single piece by the use of a wide variety of metals which he
applied in masterly *zōgan* inlay techniques to produce a spectacular effect. For the
main metal he employed *shakudō*, brass, and bronze in addition to iron, and as well
as making ordinary flat guards he made very skillful use of the irregular edge illustrated in plate 113 (see also pl. 97). He was also influenced by earlier styles, for
example the Hōan wheel, which he reproduced in more refined form (pl. 114).

HIRATA DŌJIN

The use of enamels in the decoration of sword fittings also began in the Momoyama
period. Enameling was practiced in the Nara period, but its use on sword fittings
appears to postdate Hideyoshi's two expeditions to Korea, although there is no firm
evidence on this point. Hirata Hikoshirō, also called Dōjin (often pronounced Dōnin),
was a native of Kyoto and the founder of the Hirata line. His boldly executed depic-
tions of auspicious objects such as the mantle of invisibility, the magic sack of longev-
ity, and the good-luck mallet and other designs were executed in *shippō-zōgan*, an
inlay technique in which colored vitreous enamels are melted together in recesses cut

158

115. Sword guard in Ko-Shōami style with pierced *futatsudomoe* ("two comma") design. Iron with gold inlay. D. 8.3 cm. Late Muromachi or Momoyama period. Tokyo National Museum.

for them in the ground metal of the *tsuba* or other fitting, using opaque enamels on some pieces and on others clear enamels underlaid with gold. The ground metal is usually iron or *shakudō*, but there are also examples made from *shibuichi*, a light or dark pickled alloy of copper and silver. A few of Dōjin's guards are signed *Hikoshirō*, but his other work—such as his *kozuka*, the handles for daggers carried in the scabbard of the main sword, and his *menuki*, small fittings under the wrapping of the hilt—is unsigned. Pieces by later members of the school are often signed *Hirata*, followed by the name of the individual concerned. However, since many of them are not in typical Hirata style, it seems that Hirata craftsmen made a point of signing their pieces whenever their identity as Hirata work was not otherwise apparent (pls. 98–102).

THE KO-SHŌAMI SCHOOL

From the end of the Muromachi period and right through the Momoyama and Edo periods the various Shōami schools, which began in Kyoto, exercised an overwhelming influence on other schools of sword-fitting makers throughout Japan. Since there are no signed pieces among the group of *tsuba* usually called Ko-Shōami ("Old Shōami"), it is unfortunately impossible to define the Ko-Shōami style with absolute accuracy. But a number of distinguishing features may be pointed out. Ko-Shōami *tsuba* are made from iron, with or without piercing, and are decorated with antique designs in *nunome zōgan*, a technique in which gold (or silver) leaf or wire is hammered into narrow grooves cut with a chisel in the main metal. Often some of the inlaid metal has been lost, as in plate 115, either because the grooves were too shallow or because the artificial black rusting, which prevents the development of natural red rust, was not properly carried out.

159

116. Sword guard with pierced design of mist and cherry blossoms. Signed *Matashichi* in gold inlay. Iron. D. 8.0 cm. Early seventeenth century. Eisei Bunko, Tokyo.

THE SCHOOLS OF HIGO PROVINCE

The schools of Higo province, the most important of which are the Kasuga, Hirata, Shimizu, and Nishigaki, flourished throughout the Edo period, stimulated by the patronage of the Hosokawa family, who took over the fief of Kumamoto in Higo in 1632. The founder of the Kasuga school, Hayashi Matashichi (pls. 96, 116), was one of the greatest of all sword-fitting makers, distinguished by the excellence of his forging and pierced work and his highly original inlay technique. Hirata Hikozō is noted for extensive use of *yamagane* (a dark impure copper) and copper and his elegant and sparing use of enamel inlays (pl. 98). Shimizu Jingo (pls. 117, 118) and Nishigaki Kanshirō were both pupils of Hikozō. Shimizu Jingo's preferred technique was bold brass high-relief inlay on iron, while Nishigaki Kanshirō specialized in the combination of pierced work and inlay typical of the Kasuga school. In all four schools the quality of work declines in the later generations but towards the end of the Edo period the Kasuga school was revived by the Kamiyoshi family whose most famous members are Fukanobu and Rakuju (pl. 119), who ranks second only to Matashichi in the quality of his craftsmanship. Fittings made by these later craftsmen can be identified by their combination of pierced work and inlay which derives from Hayashi Matashichi. Swords mounted exclusively in Higo fittings, called *Higogoshirae*, are strikingly sober, restrained, and yet warlike in appearance and are admired by connoisseurs for their sophisticated simplicity.

117. Sword guard with design of falcon in a pine tree. By Shimizu Jingo. Iron and brass. D. 7.5 cm. Early Edo period. Tokyo National Museum.

118. Sword guard with cock design. By Shimizu Jingo. Iron and brass. D. 7.5 cm. Late seventeenth century. Collection of Kishida Yūsaku.

119. Sword guard with pierced design of grasses, dewdrops, and the moon. Signed *Rakuju* in gold inlay. Iron with gold overlay. D. 8.2 cm. Eisei Bunko, Tokyo.

161

120. *Mitokoromono* with peach branch design. By Gotō Sōjō. *Shakudō*. L. of *kōgai* 21.3 cm. Late Muromachi period. Tokyo National Museum.

121. *Mitokoromono* with shell and seaweed design. By Gotō Jōshin. *Shakudō* and gold. L. of *kōgai* 21.3 cm. Late Muromachi period. Tokyo National Museum.

THE GOTŌ SCHOOL

The Gotō family of carvers were in the service of the shogunal house. The founder of the family was Yūjō, who worked for the Ashikaga shogun Yoshimasa (1435–90), and his descendants continued to serve the Ashikaga family, later receiving the patronage of Nobunaga and Hideyoshi during their respective periods of power. Gotō Tokujō, the fifth of the line, was taken into the service of Tokugawa Ieyasu. Subsequently the family flourished in the shogunal service until the Meiji Restoration of 1868, and there were a number of successful subschools which worked for daimyo all over the country.

The rules of the Gotō style, called *iebori*, "house" or "family" carving, were laid down from Yūjō's time onwards: the use of metals other than *shakudō* and gold was forbidden and the range of subject-matter, which consisted chiefly of *shishi* (stylized lionlike animals of Chinese origin), dragons, flowers, and grasses, scenes from the Nō drama, and human figures, did not leave much scope for freedom and originality of treatment.

Gotō work often comes in the form of *mitokoromono* (literally, "things for three places"), sets consisting of *menuki*, *kozuka*, and *kōgai*. The *menuki* are placed under the wrapping on either side of the hilt. Although originally intended to prevent the hands from slipping they later became an almost purely decorative feature. The *kozuka* is the handle of a small knife carried in a slot cut in the scabbard of the main sword and used for a variety of purposes (sometimes the term is applied to the whole knife). This too became predominantly decorative as did the skewerlike *kōgai*, which was carried on the other side of the scabbard. The two smaller holes which are often found on either side of the main hole for the sword in *tsuba* admit the ends of these *kozuka* and *kōgai*, which project beyond the top of the scabbard.

The successive masters of the Gotō school made a large number of *mitokoromono* with a *shakudō* ground worked in the regular granulation called *nanako* decorated in gold or *shakudō*. The various *mitokoromono* illustrated here in plate 103 and in plates 120–23 are by Sōjō, the second master; Jōshin, the third master; Tokujō, the fifth master; Renjō, the tenth master; and Enjō, the thirteenth master.

122. *Mitokoromono* with *shishi* (lion-dog) design. By Gotō Tokujō. *Shakudō* and gold. L. of *kōgai* 21.3 cm. Momoyama or early Edo period. Tokyo National Museum.

123. *Mitokoromono* with design of the twelve animals of the zodiac. By Gotō Mitsutaka (Enjō). *Shakudō* and gold. L. of *kōgai* 21.2 cm. Mid-Edo period. Tokyo National Museum.

YOKOYA SŌMIN

Dissatisfaction with the rigidly traditionalist and mannerist tendencies of the Gotō school, led, in the latter half of the Edo period, to the introduction by Yokoya Sōmin, who started his career as an assistant in the Gotō workshops, of the *machibori*, or "urban carving," style. In his freely conceived, lively, and even extravagant creations, filled with a freshness quite alien to the work of the Gotō school, he successfully broke out of the stylistic impasse which *iebori* had reached, introducing a new realism, as illustrated by the *kozuka* with *shishi* and peony design in plate 104, and showing a new interest in the real world. His fresh approach had a strong appeal not only for the great merchants but also for the daimyo and the higher ranks of the samurai.

THE NARA SCHOOL

The Nara school—based in Edo and not connected to the centuries-old city of Nara—rose to fame at about the same time as the Yokoya school founded by Sōmin, and its principal members, Sugiura Jōi, Nara Toshinaga, and Tsuchiya Yasuchika, are known as the *Nara no sansaku* ("Three Great Masters of the Nara School"). Jōi specialized in *kozuka* and in *fuchi-kashira*, the fittings for either end of the hilt, and he invented the technique of *shishiaibori*, or relief carving below the level of the main ground of the piece. Toshinaga produced very few pieces but some of his guards are masterpieces, and he was a skillful exponent of the *takabori iroe* technique in which designs are modeled in high relief in a metal different from that used for the body of the *tsuba* and additionally decorated with inlay of other metals. A typical example of his work is the guard design based on the story of Ōmori Hikoshichi and the witch, taken from the *Taiheiki*, a fourteenth century historical work. It is a thick iron piece, square-shaped with rounded corners, showing in the right-hand half of the obverse Hikoshichi carrying the witch, whose garment of fish scales is represented by gold tinted in various shades (pl. 124). The design is continued in the bottom left-hand corner of the reverse, where we see Hikoshichi's left foot and the scabbard of his *tachi*. The artistic value of this bold and original piece, in which an incident from the *Taiheiki* was used for the first time as the subject for a sword fitting, is probably best appreciated if we look at it in isolation from its practical function. It is not seen to such good effect when mounted on a sword.

124. Sword guard with design based on story of Ōmori Hikoshichi and the witch. Signed *Toshinaga*. Iron. D. 7.6 cm. Eighteenth century. Collection of Taguchi Teruo.

In 1703 Yasuchika, the last of the three masters, moved from Shōnai, at that time an obscure village in remote Mutsu province, to Edo, where he achieved great success (pls. 125, 126). His work is characterized by an exceptionally wide range of subject-matter and the use of a large number of metals, including iron, *shakudō*, copper, brass, and *shibuichi*. He was a great craftsman whose pieces in pictorial style rival those of Kaneie, while his pieces with overall design bear comparison with the works of Umetada Myōju. He appears to have made no *kozuka*. His *tsuba* are often octagonal in shape.

GOTŌ ICHIJŌ AND KANŌ NATSUO

Gotō Ichijō and Kanō Natsuo were the two principal masters of the late Edo and early Meiji periods; Ichijō was the last great member of the Gotō school, while Natsuo was the last great exponent of the *machibori* style. Ichijō was a scion of the Hachirobei subschool of the Gotō but he refused to follow unquestioningly the Gotō style and developed a realistic manner of his own, although even at the close of his life he had still not broken entirely free from Gotō traditions. One of his most striking departures

166

125. Sword guard with design of
wild boar. Signed *Yasuchika*. Iron.
D. 9.0 cm. Early eighteenth century.
Eisei Bunko, Tokyo.

126. Sword guard with design of
the arch of Aridōshi Shrine, Osaka.
Signed *Yasuchika*. Iron, with other
metals. D. 9.1 cm. Early eighteenth
century. Collection of Miyazaki
Tomijirō.

167

127. Sword guard with design of Futami-gaura bay near Ise and, on the reverse, a crane and Shinto staff. Signed *Gotō Hokkyō Ichijō*. Raised inlay on *shakudō*. D. 8.0 cm. Late Edo period. Tokyo National Museum.

from canonical tradition was his use of iron, which was strictly forbidden in the main family. Yet the fact that he signed his work in iron with special names such as Hakuō or Totsuōsanjin rather than Ichijō (which, with its *-jō* suffix, has strong Gotō connotations) indicates that he still paid superficial respect to time-honored regulations (pl. 127).

Natsuo, on the other hand, was entirely free from the bonds of tradition; he was a thoroughgoing realist whose work exhibits great freshness and originality (pls. 128, 129). His work is typically in high-relief iron, with other metals used sparingly to great effect. Ichijō died in 1876 at the age of eighty-six, but in that year Natsuo, who was only forty-nine, was at the height of his powers. Unfortunately, the revolutionary edict forbidding the wearing of swords, referred to previously, was promulgated in the same year and put a stop to the craft to which Natsuo had devoted his life. Afterwards he became an advisor to the newly established Imperial Mint, planning the design and production of gold and silver coinage, and also served as professor at the Tokyo Art School, where he brought into being the metalworking tradition of the present century. He died in 1898 at the age of seventy-one.

128. Sword guard with bamboo design. Signed *Natsuo*. Iron. D. 8.0 cm. Late Edo period. Collection of Wakayama Takeshi.

129. Sword guard with white plum design. Signed *Natsuo*. Raised inlay on iron. D. 7.4 cm. Late Edo period. Tokyo National Museum.

5

THE MAKING OF A JAPANESE SWORD

The techniques of forging which were evolved by the Japanese smith are unique and can bear comparison with those in any other part of the world. From eariiest times the functional attributes sought in a Japanese blade have been unbreakability, rigidity, and cutting power. The more purely aesthetic qualities sought by modern collectors might seem to be at variance with these severely practical requirements but in fact it is in its fulfillment of demanding technical norms that the essential beauty of a Japanese sword lies. It is obvious that unsnappability depends on the iron being soft while rigidity depends on its being hard, as does cutting power. However if the iron is hard it will snap easily and if it is soft it will not cut well. The combination of these contradictory qualities is the greatest achievement of Japanese forging and tempering techniques, whose three most important characteristics are as follows:

(1)   A hard outer skin is formed by folding over and hammering out the same piece of metal many times. This process aids the elimination of such impurities as phosphates and sulphates and also produces many layers (sometimes as many as one million) of metal of differing structure.

(2)   A softer inner core is formed by a different process of folding, using steel of lower carbon content, and the hard outer skin is wrapped around it.

(3)   A *hamon* is formed by covering the entire blade in a clay containing charcoal ash which is scraped away, in some places partially and in others completely, from the edge of the blade in the desired outline prior to heating. The varying thickness of the clay results in varying rates of cooling when the blade is quenched and these varying rates of cooling produce different crystalline compounds of iron and carbon; in particular the rapid cooling of the edge produces a hard martensitic crystalline structure while the slower cooling of the rest of the blade produces a softer pearlitic structure.

These three techniques are the most characteristic and distinctive parts of the process; also important are the shaping of the blade, the preparation of a well-formed tang, and the chiseling of the smith's signature.

Traditional accounts of the manufacture of the blade vary greatly and are often couched in deliberately mysterious language. The more detailed technical outline given below, based on the methods employed by contemporary smiths, is roughly applicable to most of the various forging procedures which have been evolved over the centuries.

Forging of the Outer Skin

(1) The smith heats a piece of good-quality steel, hammers it out into a rectangular shape, and welds it onto a long iron bar (pl. 130).

(2) Taking a separate piece of steel, weighing approximately 4.5 kilograms, the smith hammers it out flat and then breaks it into small pieces of roughly equal size. This helps to remove any remaining slag and ensures an even distribution of the second steel in the rectangular bar (pl. 131).

(3) The smith can, if he wishes, make his own individual steel out of scraps of old iron. This, too, is broken into small pieces.

(4) The smith piles the small pieces of metal onto the rectangular shape described in stage (1). He heats the whole and lightly hammers it out until it forms a single four-sided block of steel.

(5) Using increasingly heavy strokes, the smith hammers out the block into a flat plate. He scores a line with a chisel across the center of the plate, folds the metal over on itself, and then hammers the piece out again into a flat plate of the same size as before. He scores a second line at a right angle to the first and then again folds the plate over and hammers it out (pls. 132, 133). As a result of this process, which the smith repeats from ten to twenty times, impurities are forced out of the metal and the piece gradually loses weight, eventually coming down to about 950 grams. (This particular method of forging is called *jūmoji-kitae*—"forging in the shape of the character *jū*"—because the character *jū*, meaning "ten," consists of two straight lines intersecting at right angles.) The process of folding over and hammering out has three effects. First, the metal is made consistent throughout. Second, impurities are removed, resulting in steel of high quality. Third, the grain of the *ji*, referred to frequently throughout this book, is produced. This grain, be it *itame*, *mokume*, *nashiji*, or any other, makes an important contribution to the aesthetic quality of each sword.

Manufacture of the Soft Iron Core

The smith adds a small quantity of steel to the soft iron used for making kitchen knives. He then folds over the whole and hammers it out several times, during which process the weight is reduced by about two-thirds.

171

130. Materials for sword-making. RIGHT: *tamahagane*, a steel derived from iron sand. LEFT: steel for making kitchen knives.

MANUFACTURE OF THE BLADE

(1)   The smith wraps the soft iron core in the hard outer skin and then heats and hammers out the resulting assembly into a long bar of rectangular section (pl. 134).

(2)   He cuts off a triangular piece from this long bar and, again, by a process of heating and hammering the truncated area, forms the point of the blade, the *kissaki* (pl. 135).

(3)   By further heating and hammering he makes one side of the bar thin, creating the edge, gives the blade a curve, and determines the general shape of the sword and the distribution of metal within it (pl. 136).

(4)   Using a scraper and file, the smith gives the blade its final shape and polishes it roughly.

(5)   The smith covers the entire blade in a heat-resistant mixture of clay and ash called *yakibazuchi*, which he then scrapes away or thins along the edge with a metal spatula (pl. 137). The outline formed by the area of the edge thus exposed results in the pattern of the temper-line, the *hamon* (*suguha*, *midareba*, etc.), of the finished sword. In the old days clay from Mount Inaba in the Fushimi district of Kyoto was considered the best for this purpose, but any sticky clay is suitable. To it was added charcoal dust, rough polishing sand, and the like, and there were many individual formulas which were closely guarded secrets of the smith or school which used them, the aim being always to achieve a mixture which adhered well to the blade.

(6)   The clay covering of the blade is thoroughly dried and the smithy is made dark. The smith places the blade, with the clay still on it, in the furnace. The metal glows red hot, and at the moment the smith can see from its color that exactly the right temperature has been reached he takes the blade and plunges it briefly into a trough of water (pl. 138). This is the most critical stage in the entire manufacturing process and demands from the smith the highest technical skill as well as a close physical and spiritual affinity with the blade. There are a great many secret traditions affecting the temperature of the fire and the water but in fact the most critical of all

131. Hammering the separate piece of steel prior to breaking it into small pieces.

factors is the temperature of the blade itself at the moment of tempering. The manner in which the tempering is carried out determines whether the *ji* will be hard or soft, and if clay falls off the blade during the process the result is an ugly temper-line and unsightly spots in the *ji*. Careless tempering will also cause cracks to develop in the edge. This is of course fatal to any sword and renders useless all the other efforts which went into its manufacture. The tempering process is also important in that it adds an extra, natural, curve to the blade.

(7)   If this natural curve is excessive or if the tempering process bends the blade the smith can correct the fault with a hammer. If the curve is too shallow or is not as the smith intended he can alter it by putting the sword in a bronze clamp.

Finishing the Blade

(1)   If the curve is satisfactory the smith can adjust the thickness of metal in the *ji* and the edge by rough polishing, check the quality of the tempered edge, and examine the blade for flaws. He should in fact continue the finishing process down to the final polishing and the testing of the edge on bales of straw or similar material, but few modern smiths are capable of carrying out these different stages and they usually only go as far as the rough polishing.

(2)   When the smith is satisfied with the blade he shapes the tang, drills the *mekugiana*, and carefully adds his own characteristic *yasurime*, or filemarks.

(3)   Finally he engraves with a chisel his name and perhaps the date or the name of the person for whom he has made the sword.

The swordsmith's task ends at this point. Now he passes the blade on to a specialist polisher who gives it a clear bright finish. It is at this point that the sword can be considered an art object for the first time. The cooperation of other specialists, such as the makers of *habaki* sleeves and *shirasaya* (plain wood scabbards for storage) is also essential.

173

132. Hammering out and folding over.

133. Hammering out and folding over (*continued*).

134. Shaping the blade.

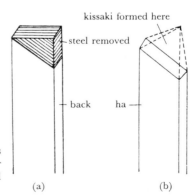

kissaki formed here

steel removed

back   ha

(a)   (b)

135. A triangular wedge is removed and the tip of the bar of metal is then hammered out to form the *kissaki*.

136. Shaping the blade (*continued*): one side is made thin and the point is formed.

137. Scraping away the mixture of clay and ash.

138. Tempering.

6

SWORD APPRAISAL

The fact that in former times the Japanese sword was called "the soul of the samurai" and held in high spiritual esteem did not prevent the manufacture of large numbers of fakes. We should not, however, jump to the modern conclusion that all these fakes were made with malicious intent, for during the feudal period family status and convention were of such immense importance that fakes were something of a necessity of daily life.

For example, it was regarded as essential that those of the court noble families (the *kuge*) which traced their descent from the five branches of the Fujiwara clan should possess an example of the work of Sanjō Munechika, but swords by Munechika were extremely rare and even if available could only be bought for a very high price. Furthermore, matters were made worse by a change in fashion among these families during the Momoyama and Edo periods. Previously they had worn swords only for decorative effect (unlike the samurai, who wore them for practical use) as may be gathered from the fact that until the Muromachi period the *tachi* mountings which they wore often contained a simple piece of hammered-out iron instead of a real blade. However, during the Momoyama and Edo periods, they took to following the military families (the *buke*) in wearing genuine blades inside their *tachi* mountings. Since it was essential to own a Munechika, in order to advertise the quality of the *tachi* handed down in one's family, it was quite natural that the signature *Munechika* should be added to swords or that swords with the signature should be specially manufactured to meet this need. Again, no daimyo family could be without *tantō* by Masamune and Awataguchi Yoshimitsu. Since the name of Masamune was synonymous in Japan with the idea of *meitō* every daimyo family found it necessary to have one of his blades in its treasury, and because the *tantō* of Yoshimitsu were said to protect their owners it was vital to have one of them as well.

For the three hundred daimyo families of the Edo period each to possess blades by Yoshimitsu and Masamune it would have been necessary for three hundred genuine blades by each smith to have been in existence. But it is clear that nothing like this number was available even at the time, since in the *Kyōhō meibutsuchō* only thirty-four blades by Yoshimitsu and fifty-nine by Masamune are listed, and in each case eighteen blades are in the section reserved for pieces which were known to have existed at some time but had been lost in fires by the time of compilation. Furthermore, even in these small totals there are some blades which, in the light of more recent research, are no longer considered genuine. Of course there existed some blades by Yoshimitsu and Masamune which did not qualify as *meitō*, but even if we include these there would be nothing like enough blades to satisfy the requirements of the daimyo. In order to meet their needs, therefore, there was no solution other than to manufacture the requisite quantity of Yoshimitsu and Masamune blades. Moreover, since there was, at the time, no such thing as a rigorous and scholarly attitude towards the identification of art objects, if a sword possessed by a daimyo family was traditionally regarded as the work of Masamune there was no reason why people should dismiss it as a fake or a forgery, and indeed such conduct would have been quite unthinkable.

When a succession took place in the shogunal family it was customary for daimyo throughout Japan to present a *tachi*, *katana*, or *tantō* with the signature *Kunimitsu*, the characters for which can be taken as meaning "may the fortunes of the nation prosper," by way of congratulation. The most famous Kunimitsus were of course Rai Kunimitsu and Shintōgo Kunimitsu, but since the work of both these smiths is comparatively rare, it became quite usual to secure a blade which had lost its signature through shortening, have a certificate (*origami*) made out stating that it was the work of Rai Kunimitsu or Shintōgo Kunimitsu, and present it to the new shogun. As a result there are today a great many Kunimitsu blades in many different styles in existence, some of which have even had the signature added. Just as the daimyo had no qualms about presenting these blades to the shogun, so the shogun was happy to accept them without inquiring as to their authenticity, and it was also quite usual for them to be presented back by the shogunal family to the daimyo from whom they had been received on suitable occasions.

When traditionally important birthdays, for example the sixty-first, seventieth, or seventy-seventh, came round it was customary to present *tachi* and *katana* with signatures such as *Toshinaga* and *Enju*, which can be taken to mean "long life," or even *Chiyozuru*, meaning "a crane which lives for a thousand seasons." Of course some of these blades with auspicious signatures were genuine but it cannot be denied that a good many of them were no more than fillers for the mounts in which they came. In any case, provided the gift was auspicious there was absolutely no need for anyone to look too closely into the authenticity or otherwise of its signature.

After the law of 1876 abolishing the wearing of swords and the gradual intensification of economic activity during the early Meiji period there prevailed a mistaken assumption that because a sword was said to be a Munechika which had been passed down in a noble family or a Masamune which was the heirloom of a daimyo house, it automatically qualified as a *meitō*. Real *meitō* were not, of course, to be found in the possession of townsmen or ordinary samurai but it is obvious that it cannot be

177

conversely assumed that all swords possessed by important families, whatever their signature, are necessarily *meitō*. The ignorance concerning swords which characterized the Meiji period tragically opened up a wide field for the activities of unscrupulous dealers. Such people had operated at all periods, for wherever there are celebrated art objects there will be fakes and it is possible to do business without staking much money by peddling such things. And since there are always people who expect to make an enormous profit on a small outlay there will always be dishonest thieves willing to cater to their needs.

In the Edo period fakes purporting to be the work of famous smiths such as Nagasone Kotetsu of Edo and Tsuta Sukehiro of Osaka were made even while those smiths were still manufacturing blades themselves. The business of faking has been going on for three centuries, but it is a matter for concern that counterfeiting techniques have of late made prodigious progress, and modern examples, unlike the almost charming and innocuous fakes of former times, have gradually come to bear an alarming resemblance to the real thing. This is due both to rapid technological developments and to recent progress in the methodical study of old swords and the precise analysis of individual styles and signatures.

For example, it used to be very difficult to "age" a false signature by rusting it, because artificially induced rust was the wrong color and could easily be detected. Using modern techniques it is now quite simple to produce what looks like three or four centuries' rust in a few days. Even more worrying is the practice of removing the tang from a blade which has a good signature but is otherwise worn out or flawed and attaching it to a good-looking blade in the appropriate style which is unsigned or has lost its signature. The practice was known in the Edo period but examples of that date are almost childishly crude, and easy to detect upon close examination. The two joining techniques employed in the Edo period are shown in plate 139, in which the blade is viewed from above with the back upwards. However skillfully such joins are made they can always be seen in the back even if they are invisible on the flat sides.

Nowadays, when the tang is joined by electrical welding the faking is less easy to detect. But electrically welded tangs do have certain visible characteristics which are shown in plate 140. When the tang is welded electrically the join is not made in the area of the *mekugiana* as it would have been traditionally, but in the usually shiny area immediately below the *hamachi* and *munamachi*. This is done so as to preserve the rusty appearance of the tang. In order to disguise the weld it is necessary to add a certain amount of rust to cover the transitional area between blade and tang. If the rust in the area immediately below the *habakimoto* has a peculiar, blotchy appearance the blade as a whole should be treated with great caution.

Uneven-looking filemarks in the same area are another suspicious sign. In order to prevent the *yakidashi* (the end of the *hamon*) from being altered by heat during the welding process, the join is often made quite far down the new blade, resulting in

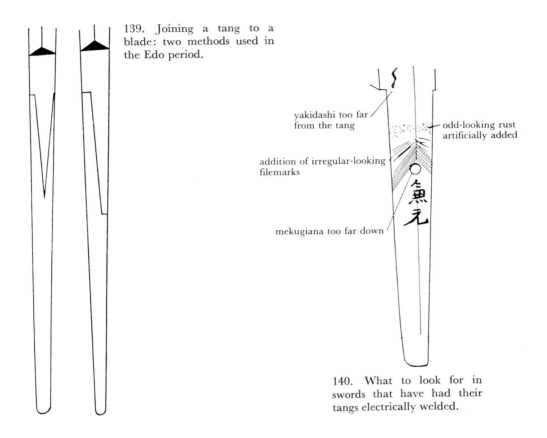

139. Joining a tang to a blade: two methods used in the Edo period.

yakidashi too far from the tang

odd-looking rust artificially added

addition of irregular-looking filemarks

mekugiana too far down

140. What to look for in swords that have had their tangs electrically welded.

excessive distance between the *hamachi* and *munamachi* and the *mekugiana*, while on the other hand the unnatural absence of *yakidashi*, due to the heating, is another feature of swords with joined tangs which should also be watched for. Electrically welded tangs can be detected scientifically by X-ray.

RETEMPERING

Retempering is another very important feature to look out for when appraising sword blades. This occurs where a blade has lost its tempered edge through fire or excessive polishing and someone other than the original smith creates an entirely new sword by retempering it. Such retempering can make a sword suitable for practical use again but it totally destroys its importance as an art object. For example if a *tachi* signed "Made by Nagamitsu of Osafune in Bizen province" has been retempered, no matter how splendid and authentic its signature it can no longer be regarded as the work of Nagamitsu and if, as is unlikely, the name of the retemperer is known, it cannot be regarded as his work either. There are, however, certain exceptions. If the shape of the blade is completely unaltered and undamaged, the main body is good, the retempering is close to the style of the original smith, the blade is old, and the works of the original smith are rare, it can, even though retempered, be officially classified as an Important Art Object or even, if it occupies a notable position in the history of the Japanese sword, as an Important Cultural Property. Nonetheless, the fact that it has been retempered cannot be ignored and it certainly lessens its artistic value.

179

It is easy to be misled by a retempered blade and the following points should, therefore, be noted:

(1) Sometimes the shape or curve of the tang is severely affected. Blades in this class include those with a very strong or very weak curve which does not appear to correspond to the known style of any particular period.

(2) Sometimes the metal of retempered blades is very dull or unusually bright. These unusually bright blades should be carefully distinguished from certain works of second-class smiths of the Shinshintō period which have a type of bright metal called *hadamono-zukuri* ("flashy make").

(3) Blades featuring *muneyaki* with the signature of a smith whose work is not characterized by this effect should be treated with suspicion.

(4) *Hamon* which appear to be in a more recent style than the period of the smith whose signature appears on the tang or which lack firmness and brightness often indicate that a blade has been retempered but are difficult to distinguish without considerable experience. A dull *hamon*, whose outline resembles that of characters drawn on wet paper, is also seen in blades which have been subject to excessive and repeated polishing and it is necessary to determine whether it is polishing or re-tempering which has caused the dullness.

(5) There are different and distinctive styles of *hamon* depending on period, school, and province, and the *hamon* of famous smiths have in addition a marked individual character. Distinctive and individual styles are not found in retempered *hamon*. For example, Bizen blades of the mid-Kamakura period are noted for their *chōji hamon* made up of *nioi*. If a blade signed *Nagamitsu* has *hitatsura hamon* or *gunome hamon* made up of *nie*, it is suspect.

(6) In the appraisal of swords the *yakidashi* and *bōshi* are the most important areas. The condition of the *yakidashi* is especially useful in determining whether or not a blade has been retempered. For example, if a sword has been shortened and yet its *yakidashi* still starts from the *hamachi*, it must have been retempered (see pl. 141). If a Shintō-style straight *yakidashi* is seen in a Kotō blade, this in itself is enough to indicate retempering. In Kotō blades, the effect called *yakiotoshi* in which the *hamon* starts above the *hamachi* is quite common and is especially distinctive of Kyushu blades and above all those of Bungo province. However, it is also seen in retempered blades, where the tempering is often started at some distance above the *hamachi* in order to avoid damaging the rusty appearance of the tang (see pl. 142). In the case of re-tempered blades there is also often a shaded area sloping diagonally upwards from *ha* to *mune* at the beginning of the *hamon*, called *mizukage*. It appears as a whitish patch at about 45° to the line of the blade. A clear distinction should be drawn between the *mizukage* effect and the whitish reflections which appear at the beginning of the *hamon* of all blades. It should also be remembered that for some reason *mizukage* which are not due to retempering appear in the work of the Horikawa school and the school of Hizen Tadayoshi.

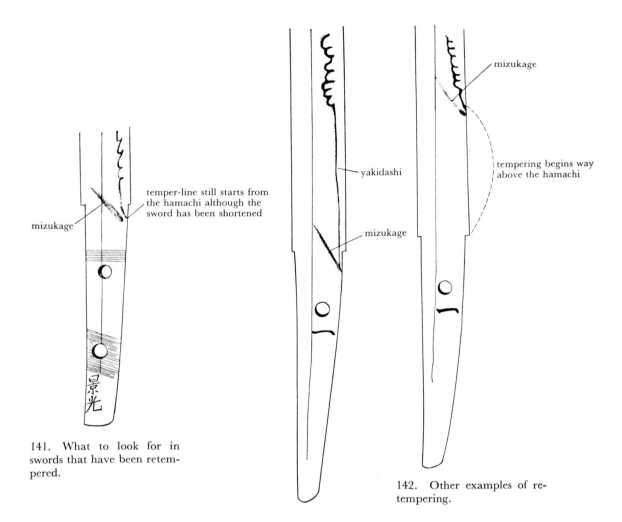

141. What to look for in swords that have been retempered.

142. Other examples of retempering.

mizukage

temper-line still starts from the hamachi although the sword has been shortened

mizukage

yakidashi

mizukage

mizukage

tempering begins way above the hamachi

(7) *Bōshi*, too, are an important test of a smith's skill and the *bōshi* of *meitō* are all outstanding in their individual way while those of retempered blades have little merit. If the *bōshi* does not correspond to the known style of the smith or is stiff and rigid in outline it is a bad sign and can be an important factor in determining whether a blade has been retempered or not.

(8) When retempering has taken place it often happens that although the main part of the sword is skillfully executed the rust of the tang loses its refined and antique appearance and the blade as a whole looks rather dry. This too is a phenomenon whose significance is hard to assess in individual cases without considerable experience. But if the surface of a blade seems dry and hard even after liberal applications of oil, it is probable that it has been retempered. A greenish tinge is another suspect sign which can by itself enable the appraiser to determine that a blade has been retempered.

Although the features which indicate retempering have been set out individually above, it is vital that they should be taken into account collectively when judging a blade. One should avoid jumping to hasty conclusions.

SIGNATURES

Inlaid signatures of various kinds which are sometimes found on tangs are another feature which should be treated with caution. The most common of them is the *gakumei*, which occurs when a blade is shortened and a rectangular piece of metal bearing the signature is cut from the discarded portion and set in the new tang. The authenticity of such added signatures is exceedingly difficult to judge. If, taking Nagamitsu as an example again, the blade is in his style and the *gakumei* is a good one, it can be accepted without hesitation. But there are many cases where the style and the smith indicated on the *gakumei* do not correspond or where the blade is of good quality but the signature is of dubious authenticity. We should not forget that it is in the nature of *gakumei* that when shortening occurs a signature can be taken from a different blade and inlaid in the new tang. It should also be borne in mind that because false *gakumei* are more difficult to detect than ordinary false signatures it is quite common, when adding a false signature to a blade, to inlay it in the form of a *gakumei* rather than inscribe it directly onto the tang.

Sometimes a similar type of signature called *harimei* is attached to the butt of an unsigned sword, making it look like a blade which has been only slightly shortened so that the signature was not quite lost. These *harimei* can be detected by close examination of the back of the blade, where the join will be visible, but it is possible for a careless appraiser to be misled by them. *Harimei* differ from *gakumei* in that although both types of signature are inlaid *harimei* are further down the tang and lie flush with the surface in order to hide the join as much as possible. There are some *harimei* whose signatures, although taken from other swords, correspond to the style of the blade to which they are attached. Such *harimei* are fitted with the questionable intention of passing off the result as a signed blade. This measure is perhaps allowable if taken out of regret at the absence of a signature, but if a *harimei* is added with the intention of creating a signed blade, it still has to be regarded as a fake.

The *orikaeshimei* is another type of added signature which is found on shortened blades. When the blade is cut down the part bearing the signature is left attached, folded back, and then inlaid, like the *gakumei*, into a space cut in the reverse of the tang (see pl. 143). Well-executed *orikaeshimei* are absolutely acceptable but unfortunately they too have often been unscrupulously faked by taking a good signature from another sword, for example, in the case of Nagamitsu, by fixing his signature in *orikaeshimei* position on a Shintō or Shinshintō blade in the Bizen style. Such false *orikaeshimei* can be distinguished from the genuine article by the fact that the inlaid panel and the sword are not formed from a continuous piece of metal. Since an attempt is usually made to conceal this deficiency it is important to examine the butt of the tang carefully before determining the authenticity of an *orikaeshimei*. Even so, there are many cases where the *orikaeshimei* is false even though it is joined to the tang. Just as with *harimei*, fakers prefer to attach false signatures as *orikaeshimei* rather than inscribe them direct so as to make them less easily detectable. To identify such *ori-*

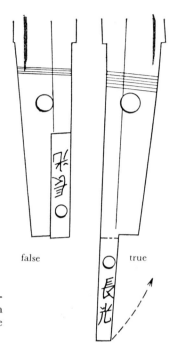

false   true

143. True and false *orikaeshi-mei*. The difference between the two can be seen at the bend.

kaeshimei it is necessary to turn the sword around, view the signature the right way up, and examine it carefully.

It is a very good idea to take a rubbing (*oshigata*) of a signature when attempting to judge its authenticity since this is often more apparent in a rubbing than in the original. In any case, there will always be something slightly suspect about the tang of a fake blade. To take a rubbing of an *orikaeshimei* or similar unorthodox signature a long piece of special rubbing paper should be folded at the butt so that it covers both sides of the tang. First of all the unsigned side of the tang should be rubbed, followed by the side with the signature. The piece of paper should then be flattened out and the two sides viewed as a whole. It will then be possible to judge whether the tang, as reconstructed in paper, is clumsily curved or has the signature in an impossible position.

It will be seen from the examples cited above that there is a regrettably wide variety of fake swords; however, the situation is much the same with other art objects and antiques and it should be emphasized that in the case of swords there is a logical method of study which facilitates the rapid discovery of fake blades and false signatures. Failure to identify these forgeries is always the result of careless or hasty judgments. It is as true for sword fittings as it is for swords that "a little learning is a dangerous thing." All doubtful or difficult pieces should be referred to experienced scholars or specialists. Another danger to watch out for is greediness. Even among true sword lovers there are those who feel compelled to make a constant search for a lucky bargain or a quick profit. The desire for personal profit is universal and need not be deplored, but if it is overindulged it can lead to serious failures of judgment. To be deceived by a fake reflects just as much on the recipient of a piece as it does on the seller. It is fatal to hanker after nothing but masterpieces with illustrious signatures or to indulge in a constant search for bargains. The best bargains are those bought for a reasonable price from a reputable dealer.

7

ESSENTIALS OF SWORD CARE

Many sword features—especially details of the *hamon*, surface textures of the steel, and signatures—are difficult if not impossible to make out without close inspection under good lighting conditions. Photographs may show some detail but they convey little sense of the metal, and at an exhibition the sword is always protected behind glass, at a distance from the viewer. To fully appreciate and study a good sword you must hold it in your hands and feel its weight, then turn it at different angles to the light and examine the grain and texture of its metal. Should you ever have the opportunity to do this, either with a sword you have purchased or with one belonging to a friend, keep the following points in mind.

A sword, if it has been properly cared for, is extremely sharp. When handling it, at all times you must exercise the greatest caution. Sudden carelessness can easily result in injury to yourself or to others, and damaging an important blade may earn you an unenviable reputation as a desecrator of cultural properties. Never touch another person's sword without his permission, and avoid waving the sword around or brandishing it unnecessarily. The main thing is to be cautious and courteous.

To remove the blade for inspection, hold the scabbard in your left hand over your left knee with the edge of the blade facing upwards; grasp the hilt from above in your right hand, and gently withdraw the sword (pl. 145). When you replace the blade, hold the scabbard as before in the left hand and slowly carry the point of the blade towards the opening; to avoid causing damage to the scabbard or the blade, ease the blade straight in without any movement to either side. When you have pushed the blade fully home, press the hilt and scabbard firmly together.

To remove the hilt, leave the blade in its scabbard and first remove the *mekugi* (this is done with the special tool shown in pl. 144). Then withdraw the blade from the scabbard as before. Transfer the hilt to the left hand; keep the edge of the blade upwards and raise the sword so that it leans back over your left forearm. Now lightly tap the top of your left hand with your right fist (pl. 146). After a few taps the hilt will loosen and you will be able to withdraw the tang. You must be careful here, for if you strike your left hand too hard the sword, especially if it is a short sword like a *tantō*, may fly uncontrolled out of the hilt.

184

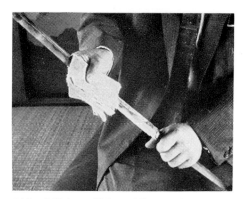

148. Wiping off the *uchiko* powder.

149. Replacing the sword in the hilt after the application of oil. By striking the base of the hilt, the tang is shaken firmly into place.

When you store your sword, avoid using a camphor-wood chest since the fumes from camphor wood can easily cause a blade to rust. However, should rust by any chance occur, get the sword to an expert polisher immediately. Amateurish efforts at correcting the damage will only make matters worse and may result in further damage that cannot be easily repaired. At one time copper coins or horn spatulas were used to rub rust away, but the effects of this technique, if unskillfully executed, are difficult to remove by polishing. It should in any case be remembered that repeated polishing is undesirable since it will result, ultimately, in the destruction of the blade. A true sword lover should be as reluctant to let his sword rust as he is to let his own body fall prey to disease.

Polishing, when it is necessary, should always be left to an expert specialist, the *togishi*. His job, like that of a beautician, is to find the good natural qualities within and make them visible without artifice. If the *togishi* is unskilled, no matter how well forged the blade he will fail to bring out its innate beauty. Worse, he can even destroy it by, for example, grinding away the ridge or creating irregularities in the surface.

A good *togishi* starts with a thorough diagnosis. He checks for rust and flaws, and he decides how he will eliminate them while at the same time showing off the blade's best qualities. To do his job properly he must bear in mind the period and style of the blade he is working on; he must be thoroughly versed in the characteristics of and the differences between, say, blades from the Kamakura period and blades in the

187

150. Polishing the back of the blade.

151. Polishing with the *nagurado* stone.

Bizen and Sagami traditions. No *togishi* who is incapable of carrying out this preliminary analysis should ever be considered competent.

The *togishi*'s goal is to restore a blade to the highest standard that its degree of rusting and general condition will permit. The basis of his polishing technique is the progressive use of abrasives of increasing fineness, starting, for example, with the coarse *iyoto* stone, removing the marks left by the *iyoto* with the *nagurado* stone, and so on, using different stones through seven or eight separate stages. During the final polishing, different methods are applied to the edge and the ground so as to produce a whitish color in the former and a bluish color in the latter (pls. 150–54).

Immediately after the *togishi* has finished, the blade will rust easily because the polishing has exposed anew the interstices between the crystals of iron and steel, allowing the penetration of water. You should therefore oil the sword two or three times a week in the way outlined above for the first two or three months until all the water has been replaced by oil. Thereafter, you need change the oil only once or twice a year barring special circumstances, although there is certainly no harm in frequent changes.

Convention dictates the manner in which swords are displayed. *Tachi* are normally displayed on stands with the hilt to the left and the blade downwards—the same

152. Polishing the *ha* with the very thin *hazuya* stone.

153. Burnishing the *shinogiji* with a metal rod.

154. Imparting a whitish color to the *bōshi*.

position as when they are worn at the waist. When the blade and its mountings are displayed together but separately, the mountings are held together by a wooden dummy blade and are usually placed below the real blade. A *tachi* mounting on a vertical stand should be placed so that the back of the scabbard faces the viewer while the hilt is at the bottom for maximum stability. Here it does not matter whether or not there is a real blade inside the mounting.

A *daishō* pair should be placed on a rack with the hilts to the left and the edges upwards, the long *katana* above the short *wakizashi*. In some old portraits of Tokugawa Ieyasu there is a sword rack mounted with swords whose hilts are to the right. It may be that this was the practice in warlike days gone by, since it would make it possible in an attack to take the scabbard in the left hand and draw the sword with the right with the minimum delay. But it may simply be an artist's error. When a *katana* is shown in an upright *tachi* stand it is customary to arrange it with the hilt upwards and the edge, as always, away from the viewer.

The important thing is to display swords effectively so that they look their best. The samurai of old may occasionally have opted for different styles according to their personal tastes, but in general their practice was in accord with the principles outlined above.

189

KOTŌ AND SHINTŌ SWORDS COMPARED

KOTŌ	SHINTŌ (INCLUDING SHINSHINTŌ)

General Shape

TACHI: Good shape, deep curve, *fumbari.* Usual length is 76–79 cm. In the mid-Kamakura period *kodachi* about 60 cm. in length were made. There are many Kotō *tachi* in existence.

UCHIGATANA: *Sakizori* and slight *fumbari.* Usual length is between 60 and 66–69 cm., but a few are as short as 48–52 cm.

TANTŌ: In the Kamakura period, *uchizori* is normal. In the Nambokuchō period, they are a little longer and have a slight curve in the normal direction (towards the back) but are still thin. In the Muromachi period there are several types, for example, the thick *takenoko-zori* style and the two-edged style. Many Kotō *tantō* exist.

TACHI: Few were made, except as copies and in the Shinshintō period. The shape is poor, often copied from a sword which had been shortened.

KATANA: Gentle curve with no *fumbari.* Usual length is 66–76 cm.

WAKIZASHI: This term is used for swords under 60 cm. in length. In form they are the same as *katana.* Usual length is 51–57 cm.

TANTŌ: A few are found in the early Shintō period or as antiquarian revivals. They are rather large, with either a slight curve or no curve at all. They often exaggerate the typical features of *tantō* of the Kotō period and are usually rather thick, with *sakizori.* Those of better quality usually date from the Shinshintō period.

Hamon

The *nioi* are tightly packed, rich, and active. The whole surface has a soft, full feel. The *ashi* are fine, active, and yet unfussy. The *nie* are bright and extravagant, yet consistent. Ostentatious features such as *kinsuji* and *inazuma,* with the strength and splendor of a black diamond, are also found. In all periods and schools, the only *hamon* found are *suguha, chōji, notare, hitatsura,* and *gunome.*

The *nioi* are loosely distributed and the tempered area is wide. There is little activity or variation in the temper-line. The *nioi* of Shinshintō are particularly fresh and clear in appearance. Typical *hamon* are either derived from classical types—*suguha, notare, gunome*—or are wildly unconventional; for example, *sudareba* ("venetian-blind" style), *tōranha* (strong waves), *juzuba* (like a string of rosary beads), *kikusuiha* (chrysanthemum blossom floating on water), *Fujimisaigyō* (priest viewing Mount Fuji), and *kobushigata* ("fist-shaped") *chōji.*

KOTŌ	SHINTŌ

Bōshi

Bōshi are firm, active, and powerful, and often conform to traditional types. The turnback is gentle and natural in appearance.

Bōshi are mostly hard-looking and rather mediocre. No matter how good the last few inches of the *hamon* of the main part of the blade, the *bōshi* is always somewhat bland and shows little activity. The end of the turnback is stiff and unnatural and shines too brightly.

Yakidashi

This part of the *hamon* near the tang is natural and unaffected. *Koshiba* (stopping several centimeters above the *hamachi*) and *yakiotoshi* (stopping somewhat nearer the *hamachi*) are frequently encountered.

The *hamon* usually straightens to *suguha* near the *habakimoto*. The contrast of *suguha* with *midareba* in the main *hamon* is common later in the period.

Grain of Metal

Various types, for example, *itame, mokume, masame,* and *ayasugihada* (gently undulating), are found at different periods. Whatever the type, the grain is bright and lively. There are many *chikei*, often in combination with mottling, and there is much activity throughout the *ji*. *Utsuri* are frequently encountered.

Itame, mokume, masame, ayasugihada, nashiji, and others are found, and sometimes a mixture of native and imported iron is used, resulting in a rather blackish appearance. By contrast, an attempt is sometimes made to imitate the whitish surface of Kotō blades, but the results are inferior to their Kotō models in quality, luster, and vitality. There are a few irregular grains peculiar to the Shintō period, and in the Shinshintō period we find a number of blades with a hard and apparently unforged surface texture known as *kagamihada*. *Chikei* effects are found but are usually the result of using an impure metal and are of no interest. *Utsuri* are occasionally found in the blades of the Ishidō school, otherwise hardly at all.

Horimono

Usually simple and bold. The subject matter is normally of Buddhist origin, for example

Horimono are fine and deep but often lack the dignity of earlier periods. When subject-

191

KOTŌ   SHINTŌ

ken (straight sword), *bonji* (stylized Sanskrit characters), *gomabashi* (pair of short narrow grooves, possibly related to the pair of chopsticks used in Shintō shrines to arrange the burning charcoal in the brazier at the altar), and *kurikara* (stylized dragon and straight sword), and characters such as *kamihotoke* ("gods and Buddhas," 神仏) are also found. As a rule they are placed unobtrusively, so as not to detract from the beauty of the shape, grain, and *hamon* of the sword itself.

matter of the type found on Kotō blades is used, the treatment is different, with a greater degree of stylization and exploitation of the variation between thick and thin, fine and coarse. Names of deities are not much used as motifs, and there are some playful new subjects, for example, Hōraizan, the Chinese Paradise of Eternal Youth; the *shōchikubai*, an auspicious grouping of pine, bamboo, and plum; and the carp leaping a waterfall, symbolic of worldly success. In the work of swordsmiths who made a specialty of them, *horimono* are rather large and placed in such a way that attention is directed towards their qualities in particular rather than to those of the blade as a whole.

Tang

In *tachi* the shape is usually *kijimomogata*, slightly curved towards the blade end. In *tantō* it is usually *furisodegata* (a kimono-sleeve shape with the edge side swelling out towards the blade), *funagata* (shaped like a Japanese fishing boat), or *tanagobara* (a bulging curved line on the blade-edge side of the tang like the belly of a fish). Filemarks are of various traditional types—*kiri, sujikai, katte sagari*—in contrast to the fancier Shintō styles. The shape of the butt should be in accordance with the style of the school concerned, for example, the *kengyō* tip (shaped in a blunt point like that of a *ken* sword) that began with Masamune of the Sagami tradition, or the *kurijiri* (chestnut shape) of Bizen.
SIGNATURES: Prior to the Muromachi period signatures on *tachi* are usually on the side facing outwards when the *tachi* is worn, i.e., slung at the left side, edge down. *Uchigatana* and *tantō* signatures are usually on the other side, i.e., the side which faces outwards when

Apart from a few eccentric forms, most tangs follow standard Kotō types. Filemarks show rather more individuality than those of Kotō tangs. Although rare in Momoyama-period blades, in the Edo period large decorative filemarks are much used. The shape of the butt exhibits, like the filemarks, a greater degree of individuality, but it is still possible to make a classification according to school, and there are often very strictly observed differences, depending on the year of manufacture, within the production of individual smiths. Generally speaking, the rounded *kurijiri* shape is most frequent in the early Edo period, later giving way to the uneven V-shaped *iriyamagata* type.
SIGNATURES: All swords, apart from *tachi* and those made in Hizen province or by Echizen Kunikiyo, have the signature on the side which faces outwards when the blade is worn, edge up. Apart from the swords of Horikawa Kunihiro and Hankei, two-character signatures are rare, the preference

KOTŌ

SHINTŌ

they are worn, edge up. *Tachi* signatures are usually of two characters only, with no further information. After the mid-Kamakura period it is quite common for the date also to be inscribed, and this is still more typical of *uchigatana* of the Muromachi period. Bizen blades of this period almost always have a date. Honorary titles are very rare indeed before the Muromachi. Later on, signatures with wholly honorary titles are found, such as *Izumi no kami* and *Wakasa no kami*.

being for longer inscriptions. In the early Edo period a date is often added and this becomes more frequent as time goes on. But this, too, is a matter of individual taste and style, and we find, for example, such examples as *Musashi no daijō Tadahiro* without the date. Both swordsmiths of the first class and those of inferior ability use honorary titles in the form *AB no kami YZ*, where *AB* is the name of a province and *YZ* is the name of the smith. *Kami* means "governor," and is a title used under the old imperial system of Chinese origin. Another such title is *daijō*, "steward." There are few exceptions to this use of honorary titles, among whom Kuniyasu, Kotetsu, and Minamoto no Kiyomaro should be mentioned.

Other General Features

Kotō swords are gentle and pleasing to handle. The shape of blade and tang, the color of the rust, and the signature are all quiet, restrained, and antique in feeling.

Shintō swords feel somewhat heavy when handled. By comparison with Kotō swords, they have something of the parvenu about them. They give one a strong impression of youth and ostentation.

LIST OF ILLUSTRATIONS IN JAPANESE

195

GLOSSARY

Many of the features of swords and their fittings are illustrated in plates 2–13 in the Introduction, and in plates 76 and 77.

aikuchi (合口; "fitting mouth"): a term used to describe all sword mountings in which there is no guard (*tsuba*) between the hilt and the scabbard. More specifically it is used as an abbreviated form of the term *aikuchi tantō*, which refers to a type of guardless dagger, often highly decorated, that was popular from the Kamakura period onwards.

ashi (足; "legs"): lines of martensitic structure projecting into the *ha* at right angles to the *hamon*.

ayasugihada (綾杉肌): one of the types of graining visible in the metal of the *ji*, resembling the regular wavy grain of the wood of the *sugi* (cryptomeria) tree.

bakufu (幕府): the military government of the shogun. The *bakufu* set up at Kamakura at the beginning of the Kamakura period (1185–1332) was responsible for the sudden rise to preeminence of the Sagami school of swordsmiths.

bonji (梵子): stylized Sanskrit characters, often used in the decorative carvings on the sides of a blade.

bōshi (帽子): the part of the *hamon* which is in the point of the blade (*kissaki*). It is particularly important to make a thorough examination of the *bōshi* when assessing a sword.

chikei (地景): brightly shining areas of curved outline occurring in the *ji*.

chōji (丁子): a type of *hamon*, having the irregular appearance of buds of the *jinchōge* plant (*Daphne odora*; clove).

chū-kissaki (中鋒): blade point (*kissaki*) of medium length in proportion to the width of the blade near the tang.

chū-suguha (中直刃): *suguha hamon* of medium width.

daishō (大小; "big-little"): the pair of long and short swords (*katana* and *wakizashi*), worn edge upwards thrust through the belt, which came into widespread use during the Momoyama period (1573–99).

Edo period (1600–1867): the period of rule of the Tokugawa shogunate, or military government, in Edo (modern Tokyo). The *daishō* pair of long and short swords came into widespread use just at the beginning of the period and because of the lasting peace, mountings became more and more elaborate and decorative. The period saw the emergence of many schools of sword-fitting makers at Edo and Kyoto and in the provinces. Many schools of eminent swordsmiths were active in the early years of this period located especially in the castle towns, notably Edo and Osaka, and in Kyoto. There was a second phase of high-quality production in the third quarter of the seventeenth century, and at the end of the eighteenth century there was a renaissance of sword manufacture led by Suishinshi Masahide, whose return to the styles of the Kamakura era ushered in the so-called Shinshintō period.

fumbari (踏張り): a term used to describe a blade which becomes noticeably wider as it approaches the hilt (i.e., a blade whose *motohaba* is considerably greater than its *sakihaba*). This is a feature of Kotō-period blades.

funagata (舟形; "boat shape"): a form of tang

said to resemble a Japanese fishing boat, broadening toward the blade.

gunome (互の目): a very common type of *hamon* markedly irregular and with sharply pointed waves.

gunome chōji (互の目丁子): a combination of *gunome* and *chōji hamon*.

ha (刃): a general term for the tempered edge of the blade. More precisely, the *yakiba* (焼刃).

habaki (鎺): a metal sleeve, often of copper-gilt, which is fitted over the area of the blade (*habakimoto*) where the tang ends and the polished part begins. It is held in place by being pressed between the notches in the edge and back of the blade (the *hamachi* and the *munamachi*) on one side and the sword guard (*tsuba*) on the other side. It serves to hold the blade tightly both in the handle and (when sheathed) in the scabbard, thus preventing possible damage and transferring the shock of any blow to the *tsuba* and hilt assembly rather than to the weak horn or bamboo pegs (*mekugi*). *Habaki* are usually not decorated with anything other than simple striations called *nekogaki* (猫搔き; "cat scratches"), designed to increase the friction holding the sword in the scabbard.

hakikake (掃きかけ): a feature of the tempered steel of the blade in which *nie* appear in a swept or brush-stroke pattern.

hamachi (刃区): the notch on the edge of a blade near the point where the polished area begins, opposite the *munamachi*.

hamon (刃文): a general term for the shape of the outline of the border between the tempered edge (the *ha*) and the untempered metal of the *ji*.

Heian period (782–1184): This period saw the establishment of imperial rule at Kyoto, followed by the rise to power of the warrior class. The most significant development in this period of sword history was the transition from the early *kissaki-moroha-zukuri* sword, which has two edges for a considerable part of its length, to the classic ridged *tachi*, exemplified in the works of the smiths Munechika, Yasutsuna, and Kanehira.

hi (樋): grooves cut in the sides of blades. They are of varying length, width, and depth and can appear singly or in pairs, on one or both sides of the blade. The way in which the *hi* terminates can sometimes be an indication of period. The *marudome* (丸留め) and more especially the *kakudome* (角留め), with rounded and squared ends respectively, are typical of the Kamakura period. The *marudome* is also commonly found in blades of the Edo period, as is the *kakinagashi* (搔流し), whose end tapers to a point. Care should be exercised in assessing the ends of *hi*, since their shape and position can be affected by shortening of the blade, and *hi* are sometimes added a long time after the manufacture of the blade. In the case of blades with their tangs intact and unaltered (*ubu*), grooves on Kotō-period swords usually come to the middle of the tang while Shintō swords tend to stop short of the *machi*.

hira-zukuri (平造り): a blade type, flat with no ridge and roughly triangular in construction.

hitatsura (皆焼): a style of tempering, introduced during the Nambokuchō period (1333–91), which leaves hard-tempered areas irregularly scattered on the surface of the blade as well as in the edge.

horimono (彫物): engraving or carvings on the sides of blades. These include grooves (*hi*) and more decorative features such as stylized Sanskrit letters (*bonji*), gods or dragons, frequently having religious significance, especially on older blades.

hososuguha (細直刃): a type of *hamon* in which the line is straight and thin.

hotsure (ほつれ): a streaky, brushed-looking area which sometimes occurs on the border of the cutting edge of a tempered blade.

ikubi-kissaki (猪首鋒): a short and stubby blade-point, said to resemble the neck of a wild boar (*ikubi*).

iorimune (庵棟): a ridged type of blade back.

197

iriyamagata (入山形): a butt with an asymmetrical V-shape.

itame (板目): the commonest of the surface textures found in the *ji*. It is said to resemble the surface of a wooden board cut against the grain.

ji (地): a general term for the surface structure of the blade between the edge (*ha*) and the ridge (*shinogi*).

jifu (地斑): a special forging pattern, made up of very fine wavy or spiral lines.

jinie (地沸): *nie* occurring in the *ji* rather than in the tempered edge (*ha*).

juzuba (珠数刃): a type of *hamon*, similar to *chōji*.

kakinagashi (掻流し). See *hi*.

Kamakura period (1185–1332): This period saw the establishment of the *bakufu* military government at Kamakura in eastern Honshu and the attempted Mongol invasions of 1274 and 1281. This was the golden age of the Japanese sword, during which the *tachi* and *tantō* reached their highest peaks of technical quality and beauty.

kammuri otoshi (冠落し): a type of sword style in which the *shinogiji*, the area on the blade between the ridge and the back (i.e., between the *shinogi* and the *mune*), is of varying width, narrowing towards the middle. Most swords have a *shinogiji* of roughly uniform width throughout.

katakiriha-zukuri (片切刃造り): a blade type, ridged on only one side and flat on the other.

katana (刀): a curved blade longer than 60 centimeters, usually around 90 centimeters long; it is worn thrust edge upwards through the belt, in contrast to the *tachi*, and is often worn in combination with shorter *wakizashi*. The *katana* came into widespread use in the early Muromachi period (1392–1572).

katte sagari yasurime (勝手下り鑢目): a type of filemark that slopes slightly toward the back of the tang.

kazaritachi (飾太刀): an elaborate style of *tachi* mounting, chiefly for court use.

ken (剣): a straight two-edged sword, used until the ninth century and rarely thereafter.

kengyō (剣形): a butt with a symmetrical V-shape.

kijimomo (雉子股; "pheasant's thigh"): a type of tang that narrows sharply on the edge side.

kinsuji (金筋): brightly shining curved threadlike areas in the edge (*ha*). They resemble *chikei*, which occur in the *ji*.

kiriha-zukuri (切刃造り): a blade type with flat sides but with an angle between the sides and the cutting edge.

kiri yasurime (切鑢目): a type of filemark that is at right angles to the length of the tang.

kissaki (鋒): a general term for the point of a blade. It is normally marked off from the rest of the blade by a transverse ridge called the *yokote*.

Ko-Bizen (古備前): the earliest school of swordmaking in Bizen province, active in the later Heian period. Its founders were Tomonari and Masatsune.

kōgai (笄): a skewerlike implement, carried in the scabbards of *katana* and *wakizashi*.

kojiri (鐺): the butt of the scabbard, often covered by a special fitting.

ko-kissaki (小鋒): blade point (*kissaki*) of short length in proportion to the width of the blade near the tang.

komaru (小丸): a type of *bōshi* (*hamon* in the blade point) that turns back at the end in a rounded hook.

konie (小沸): "small" *nie*, a feature of the metal forming the *hamon*.

koshizori (腰反り): a type of blade curve which has its center nearer the tang than the point. It is typical of early blades from late Heian to mid-Kamakura times, especially blades from Bizen province.

Kotō (古刀; "old sword"): a term used for pre-Edo-period swords. The date of transition to the Shintō ("New Sword") period is usually given as 1596.

kozuka (小柄): a small knife or, more specifically, the handle of a small knife, worn in the scabbards of *katana* and *wakizashi* on the side opposite to the *kōgai*.

kurijiri (栗尻): a butt with a rounded asymmetrical V-shape.

Kyōhō meibutsuchō (享保名物牒): a written document that appraises all the great swords (*meitō*) in Japan, compiled by the Hon'ami family in 1719 on the orders of the shogun Yoshimune.

macchi. See *hamachi*; *munamachi*

makie (蒔絵; "scattered picture"): a technique of decoration in which gold or silver powder is sprinkled onto a wet lacquer surface to form a design. Sword mountings are often decorated in *makie*.

marumune (丸棟): a rounded type of blade back.

masame (柾目): a common surface feature of the metal in the *ji*. It shows a straight grain with lines running parallel to the length of the blade.

mei (銘): the signature on the tang. The signature on a blade is one of its most important properties, and it is often preserved when a sword is shortened by resetting in a new tang (額銘; *gakumei*) or by bending the old bit of metal bearing the signature back into the newly shortened tang (折り返し銘; *orikaeshimei*). See plate 143.

meitō (名刀; "sword with a name"): a fine sword, officially recognized as such.

mekugi (目釘): a peg of bamboo or horn which passes through holes in the hilt (目釘孔; *mekugiana*) and the tang and secures the blade in the hilt.

menuki (目貫): small decorative carved metal fittings worn under the wrappings of the hilts of *katana* and *wakizashi*. They are said to improve the grip.

midareba (乱刃): a term referring to all irregular *hamon* outlines.

midarekomi (乱込み): the *midare hamon* continued into the point of the blade (*kissaki*).

mitokoromono (三所物): a set of *kozuka*, *kōgai*, and *menuki* usually in related design and for mounting on the same blade.

mitsumune (三ツ棟): a three-sided type of blade back.

mokume (杢目): a common surface feature of the metal in the *ji*, usually described as resembling a burl wood-grain.

Momoyama period (1573–99): The period dominated by the warlords Oda Nobunaga, Toyotomi Hideyoshi, and Tokugawa Ieyasu and characterized by increasing national unity and considerable contact with the West. In sword history the most important development was the establishment of the *daishō* style, the use of a pair of long and short swords (the *katana* and *wakizashi*); this marks the beginning of the Shintō ("New Sword") period.

motohaba (元幅): width of the blade where the polished part ends and the tang begins.

munamachi (棟区): the notch on the back of a blade near where the polished metal begins; it is opposite the *hamachi*.

mune (棟): a general term for the back of a blade, that is, the side opposite the tempered edge (*ha*).

Muromachi period (1392–1572): A period of almost continuous civil strife, during which the Ashikaga family were shoguns. The *katana* and *naginata* blades were increasingly preferred to the *tachi*, and all weapons were produced in very large numbers and by less exacting standards. The Seki and Bizen schools were predominant later in the period. Also, the *shakudō* copper-and-gold alloy began to be used about this time for metal sword-fittings.

nagasa (長さ): the "length" of a sword, defined as the measure of the chord joining the tip of the point and the notch on the back of the blade marking the beginning of the tang (the *munamachi*).

naginata (薙刀): a halberd, with a curved, single-edged blade.

nakago (茎): a general term for the part of a blade that is concealed inside the hilt; in English, the tang.

nakagojiri (茎尻): a general term for the end of the tang; the butt of the sword.

Nambokuchō period (1333–91): A period during which there were two rival lines of emperors. Many outsized *tachi* were made and the *naginata* was much used.

nanako (魚子): a surface treatment with the appearance of fish roe, consisting of minute hemispherical and individually punched granulations. It was much used on the copper-and-gold alloy *shakudō*.

nie (沸): hard bright areas of steel of martensitic crystalline structure, resulting from the tempering process and forming the *hamon*, by standing out in contrast to areas of softer pearlitic structure. *Nie* are individually discernible to the naked eye, in contrast to *nioi* (匂い), which are technically the same but which do not show up as discrete globules of steel without magnification and consequently appear as a mist- or cloudlike feature of the polished metal.

nioi (匂い). See *nie*.

notareba (湾れ刃): a term referring to a *hamon* outline that is wavelike, gently undulating, and more regular than *midare*.

ōsujikai yasurime (大筋違い鑢目): a type of filemark that slopes steeply toward the back of the tang.

sakihaba (先幅): width at the *yokote*, where the point (*kissaki*) is set off from the rest of the blade by a transverse ridge.

sakizori (先反り): a type of blade-curve whose center is near the point.

sambonsugi (三本杉): a type of *hamon* that is sharply undulating, with undulations in groups of three, some deeper than others.

shakudō (赤銅): an alloy of 100 parts of copper with 3 to 6 or 7 parts of gold, patinated to a blue-black color. It was much used for sword fittings and guards (*tsuba*).

shibuichi (四分一): an alloy of approximately 3 parts of copper to 1 part of silver, patinated to a variety of gray colors. It was frequently used in the making of sword guards (*tsuba*).

shinogi (鎬): the ridge on the side of a blade and running along its length, usually nearer the back (*mune*) than the edge (*ha*).

shinogiji (鎬地): the area of metal on a blade that lies between the ridge on the side (*shinogi*) and the back (*mune*).

shinogi-zukuri (鎬造り): the basic blade type, ridged.

Shinshintō (新々刀; "new-new sword"): the period in sword history running from the late eighteenth century to about 1876, when the wearing of swords was prohibited. During this time many of the older styles of sword were revived, particularly those of the Kamakura period.

Shintō (新刀; "new sword"): by convention, the period of swordmaking that extends from the end of the Kotō period (1596) to the beginning of the Shinshintō period in the late eighteenth century. During this period the *daishō* pair of long and short swords developed and the most representative smiths were those working in the Sagami, Bizen, and Mino traditions.

shōgun (将軍): title meaning something like "Generalissimo" and extracted from the emperor by a number of families of military dictators, in particular the Minamoto, the Ashikaga, and the Tokugawa.

sori (反り): general term for the curve of the blade, defined as the greatest perpendicular distance between the length (*nagasa*) and the back (*mune*).

suguha (直刃): with *midare*, the commonest of the *hamon* outlines, used to describe all temper patterns that are basically straight.

sujikai yasurime (筋違い鑢目): a type of filemark that slopes towards the back of the tang, more than *katte sagari* but less than *ōsujikai*.

sunagashi (砂流し): lines of *nie* in the *ha*, parallel to the *hamon*.

tachi (太刀): a general term for all slung swords, that is, swords worn edge downwards. In almost all cases the signature is on the side of the tang that faces away from the body when the sword is worn.

tantō (短刀): a short blade, less than 30 centimeters in length.

togari (尖り): a type of *bōshi* (*hamon* in the blade point) that turns back sharply at the end and appears pointed.

tōranha (濤瀾刃): a type of *hamon* that has a very large, irregular outline.

toriizori (鳥居反り): a type of curve whose center lies roughly in the center of the blade.

tōsu (刀子): an early type of very short knife, approximately the size of a *kozuka*.

tsuba (鐔): the sword guard, a plate of metal of varying shapes and materials but usually roughly circular in shape; it is fitted between the hilt and the collar (*habaki*) that sets off the polished blade. It is pierced with a central wedge-shaped hole for the blade and, where needed, with one or two smaller holes to admit the ends of the *kōgai* or *kozuka*.

tsurugi (剣): a straight sword, double-edged, the same shape as the *ken*.

ubu (生ぶ; "newborn"): a term used to indicate a tang whose butt and *machi* (notches marking the end of the polished portion of the blade) are in their original location and condition.

uchigatana (打刀): a long sword worn with a guard (*tsuba*), later becoming the *katana*, preceding the development of the *daishō* pair of long and short swords during the Momoyama period (1573–99).

uchizori (内反り): a type of curve that bends slightly towards, rather than away from, the cutting edge. It is usually evident in the tang of *tantō*.

utsuri (映り): a cloudy area of bright crystal-line metal bordering the *hamon* and often appearing to be a reflection of it in the *ji*. It is separated from the *hamon* by a darker area of non-reflective quality.

wakizashi (脇指): the standard short sword of the Momoyama and Edo periods, that is, from the late sixteenth to mid-nineteenth centuries. It was worn as part of the *daishō* pair, in combination with the *katana*.

yakiba (焼刃): the tempered edge of a blade.

yakidashi (焼出し): the end section of the *hamon*, near the tang.

yakiotoshi (焼落し): a style of tempering, found on many early blades, in which the *hamon* starts a little away from the tang.

yari (槍): spear.

yasurime (鑢目): a general term for filemarks on the tang. These were often added by the smith to serve as a kind of additional signature.

yō (葉): areas of martensitic structure in the *hamon*, like *ashi* but detached and leaf-shaped.

yokote (横手): the transverse ridge separating the point (*kissaki*) from the rest of the blade. It runs from the edge (*ha*) as far as the ridge.

BIBLIOGRAPHY

JAPANESE SOURCES

(selected and annotated by Susumu Kashima, with additions by the translator)

月山貞一『日本刀に生きる』東京 刀剣春秋新聞社 昭和48年 [Gassan, Sadakazu. *My Life with Japanese Swords*. Tokyo: Tōken Shunjū Shimbunsha, 1973].
Discursive autobiography by one of the most famous of contemporary smiths. [JE]

広井雄一『備前鍛冶』(日本の美術 73) 東京 至文堂 昭和47年 [Hiroi, Yūichi. *The Swordsmiths of Bizen Province*. Arts of Japan, vol. 73. Tokyo: Shibundo, 1972].
Excellent systematic account of the province's sword history. A fine example of the work of the new generation of sword scholars.

本間順治 (薫山)『正宗相州伝の流れ』(日本の美術 142) 東京 至文堂 昭和53年 [Homma, Junji (Kunzan). *Masamune and the Swordsmithing Tradition of Sagami Province*. Arts of Japan, vol. 142. Tokyo: Shibundo, 1978].
Parallels the other three works in the Arts of Japan series dealing with the "Five Traditions." Based on the author's 1961 study (see below). [JE]

————『正倉院の刀剣』東京 日本経済新聞社 昭和49年 [————. *The Swords in the Shōsō-in*. Tokyo: Nihon Keizai Shimbunsha, 1974].
One of a series dealing with the contents of the Shōsō-in repository in Nara. As well as copious illustration and comment, includes microscopic analysis of selected blades, technical information, and an excellent English glossary of sword terms.

————『正宗とその一門』東京 日本美術刀剣保存協会 昭和36年 [————. *Masamune and His School*. Tokyo: Society for the Preservation of Japanese Art Swords, 1961].
Study of the work of Masamune and his pupils, with general introduction and simple commentaries on ninety-six blades.

————『日本古刀史』東京 日本美術刀剣保存協会 昭和33年 [————. *History of the Japanese Sword in the Kotō Period*. Tokyo: Society for the Preservation of Japanese Art Swords, 1958].
Homma's doctoral thesis. A systematic study of the Japanese sword up to the end of the sixteenth century.

————・佐藤貫一 (寒山)・末永雅雄他著『日本刀大鑑』全7巻 東京 大塚巧芸社 昭和41年 [————; Satō, Kan'ichi (Kanzan); Suenaga, Masao *et al. General Survey of the Japanese Sword*. 7 vols. Tokyo: Ōtsuka Kōgeisha, 1966].
The most comprehensive account available, covering blades, mounts, and fittings with over 700 illustrations.

————・佐藤貫一 (寒山)『鐔名作集』東京 日本美術刀剣保存協会 昭和27年 [————, and Satō, Kan'ichi (Kanzan). *Collection of Tsuba Masterpieces*. Tokyo: Society for the Preservation of Japanese Art Swords, 1952].
A selection of 159 masterpieces representing the work of all the major schools from the Muromachi period to the end of the Edo period.

加島　進『刀装具』（日本の美術 64）東京　至文堂　昭和 46 年　[Kashima, Susumu. *Sword Mountings.* Arts of Japan, vol. 64. Tokyo: Shibundo, 1971].

Excellent brief account of the development of sword mountings, followed by a more detailed treatment of the various schools of metal sword-fitting makers of the Muromachi through Edo periods.

―――『鐔の美』東京　大塚巧芸社　昭和 45 年　[―――. *The Beauty of Tsuba.* Tokyo: Ōtsuka Kōgei-sha, 1970].

General introduction and commentary on 364 illustrations of examples of this most important of metal sword-fittings.

川口　陟・飯田一雄『刀工総覧』東京　刀剣春秋新聞社　昭和 50 年　[Kawaguchi, Noboru. Revised by Iida Kazuo. *General List of Swordsmiths.* Tokyo: Tōken Shunjū Shimbunsha, 1975].

Essential reference compilation with names and brief details of about 10,000 smiths. [JE]

宮崎富次郎『安親』東京　三彩社　昭和 39 年　[Miyazaki, Tomijirō. *Yasuchika.* Tokyo: Sansaisha, 1964].

Fully illustrated account of the work of the famous early eighteenth century sword-fitting maker, by a lifetime student and collector of his work.

小笠原信夫『新刀』（日本の美術 155）東京　至文堂　昭和 54 年　[Ogasawara, Nobuo. *Japanese Swords in the Shintō Period.* Arts of Japan, vol. 155. Tokyo: Shibundo, 1979].

First-class up-to-date and original account of the later period, with full historical background followed by detailed illustrated discussion. [JE]

―――『刀剣大和と美濃』（日本の美術 137）東京　至文堂　昭和 52 年　[―――. *The Swordsmiths of Yamato and Mino Provinces.* Arts of Japan, vol. 137. Tokyo: Shibundo, 1977].

Excellent clear account, fully illustrated, of these two closely related traditions.

笹野大行『刀装具の起源』東京　日貿出版社　昭和 54 年　[Sasano, Masayuki. *The Origin of Metal Sword-Fittings.* Tokyo: Nichibō Shuppansha, 1979].

Controversial work with an ax to grind. The author believes that the *uchigatana,* the *kozuka,* and the alloy *shakudō* were all in use by the late Heian period. Captions in English as well as Japanese. [JE]

佐藤貫一（寒山）『山城鍛冶』（日本の美術 107）東京　至文堂　昭和 47 年　[Satō, Kan'ichi (Kanzan). *The Swordsmiths of Yamashiro Province.* Arts of Japan, vol. 107. Tokyo: Shibundo, 1972].

Specialist account of the Yamashiro tradition on similar lines to the present work with a general introduction followed by detailed comments on individual examples.

―――『肥後金工大鑑』東京　日本美術刀剣保存協会　昭和 39 年　[―――. *The Sword-Fittings of Higo Province.* Tokyo: Society for the Preservation of Japanese Art Swords, 1964].

A study of the sword fittings of this important provincial center, with about 500 illustrations mainly featuring the work of the Hirata, Hayashi, Nishigaki, and Shimizu schools.

島田貞良・福士繁雄・関戸健吾『刀装金工後藤家十七代』東京　雄山閣　昭和 48 年　[Shimada, Sadayoshi; Fukushi, Shigeo; and Sekido, Kengo. *Seventeen Generations of the Gotō School of Sword-Fitting Makers.* Tokyo: Yūzankaku, 1973].

The most detailed study of a sword-fitting school written to date. Copious illustrations and exhaustive biographical and stylistic accounts of the seventeen masters from Yūjō at the end of the fifteenth century to Tenjō in the middle of the nineteenth century.

203

末永雅雄『増補日本上代の武器』東京 木耳社 昭和56年 [Suenaga, Masao. *Japanese Weapons of the Early Period*. Tokyo: Mokujisha, 1981].
Revised and expanded version, taking account of new archeological evidence, of the original edition of 1934.

──── ・尾崎元春・松田権六・内藤四郎 『正倉院の大刀外装』 東京 小学館 昭和52年 [────; Ozaki, Motoharu; Matsuda, Gonroku; and Naitō, Shirō. *Tachi Mountings in the Shōsō-in*. Tokyo: Shōgakkan, 1977].
Illustrations, with comment, of the thirty *tachi* mountings in the Shōsō-in, including Chinese and Japanese examples. A variety of essays, including two technical studies by a leading modern lacquer artist (Matsuda) and metalworker (Naitō).

東京国立博物館編『日本の武器武具』東京 東京国立博物館 昭和51年 [Tokyo National Museum, ed. *Japanese Arms and Armor*. Tokyo: Tokyo National Museum, 1976].
Catalog of the most comprehensive arms and armor exhibition ever held. Fully illustrated. [JE]

若山泡沫（猛）『金工事典』東京 雄山閣 昭和47年 [Wakayama, Hōmatsu (Takeshi). *Dictionary of Sword-Fitting Makers*. Tokyo: Yūzankaku, 1972].
Essential reference compilation giving biographical details of over 5,000 craftsmen. Useful appendices with chronologies, photographs of signatures, etc. [JE]

FURTHER READING
(selected and annotated by the translator)

Armes et Armures du Japon ancien. Paris: Musée Cernuschi, 1979.
Catalog of a loan exhibition from Japan, with illustrations and discussions of many famous pieces.

Compton, Walter A.; Homma, Junji; Satō, Kanzan (Kan'ichi); and Ogawa, Morihiro. *Nippon-tō: Art Swords of Japan*. New York: Japan Society, 1976.
The catalog of an exhibition of Dr. Compton's outstanding collection, it includes, as well as very detailed catalog entries, an admirably succinct history of the Japanese sword and the best glossary currently available.

Earle, J. "The Development of the Gotō School." In *Artistic Personality and Decorative Style in Japanese Art*, edited by William Watson. Colloquies on Art and Archaeology in Asia 6. London: Percival David Foundation of Chinese Art, 1977.
An attempt at a systematic stylistic account of the official school of sword-fitting makers.

Hara, Shinkichi. *Die Meister der japanischen Schwertzieraten*. Hamburg: Lucas Gräfe, 1902; Hamburg: Museum für Kunst und Gewerbe, 1931.
Essential reference compilation on Japanese sword-fitting makers by the leading Japanese specialist of his time. Using it in conjunction with Wakayama (see Japanese list), the student can find details of nearly every maker. Both editions have their own individual merits, and the book can be used by those who know very little German.

Robinson, B. W. *The Baur Collection Geneva: Japanese Sword Fittings and Associated Metalwork.* Geneva: Collections Baur, 1980.

The latest and best in a distinguished tradition of sword-fitting catalogs by British scholars. Detailed descriptions of 2,591 pieces, with some 1,000 illustrations, organized by school, from one of the world's finest collections.

———. *The Arts of the Japanese Sword.* London: Faber and Faber, 1961, 1970.

Excellent introductory work based on traditional Japanese sources, divided into two parts, one on the blade and the other on the mounts, with a wealth of practical information for the collector. Not all the blades reproduced are nowadays regarded as authentic.

Sasano, Masayuki. *Early Japanese Sword Guards.* London: Robert G. Sawers, 1974.

Over 200 excellent illustrations. The introductory texts are valuable, but few will be able to appreciate the author's rather vague criteria for categorizing the guards.

Smith, Cyril Stanley. "A Metallographic Examination of Some Japanese Sword Blades." In *La tecnica di fabbricazione delle lame di acciaio presso gli antichi.* Milan: Centro per la Storia della Metallurgia A.I.M., 1957.

A detailed initial introductory attempt at analysis, with a wealth of microphotographs. Unimportant blades were destroyed with commendable boldness in order to obtain some of the material for this paper.

Tazawa, Yutaka. *Biographical Dictionary of Japanese Art.* Tokyo: Kodansha International, 1981.

A valuable section (pp. 575–627) of this work gives fairly detailed English accounts of all the most important swordsmiths and makers of fittings, based on the latest Japanese research.

Watson, William, ed. *The Great Japan Exhibition: Art of the Edo Period, 1600–1868,* London: Royal Academy of Arts/Weidenfeld and Nicolson, 1981.

This exhibition included a distinguished group of swords, mountings, and fittings, which are introduced and cataloged in detail.